A
GAME
OF EXTREMES
25 EXCEPTIONAL
BASEBALL
STORIES

ROY LINGSTER

A GAME OF EXTREMES

25 EXCEPTIONAL BASEBALL STORIES ABOUT WHAT
HAPPENS ON AND OFF THE FIELD

ROY LINGSTER

CONTENTS

ABOUT THE AUTHOR

Roy Lingster is a military sports instructor and the author of *The Baseball Player's Guide to Hitting Like a Pro* and *A Game of Extremes: 25 Exceptional Baseball Stories.*

Roy describes baseball as 'a hobby that got out of hand', and he's spent 25 years in the game as both player and coach. The expertise he's built throughout his career is evident in his writing, and his books provide a rich source of information and advice for baseball players who want to take their game to the next level.

Roy has been playing baseball since he was a child and spends much of his free time reading up on the sport. His knowledge continues to grow and inform his technique and coaching style.

If he had thought he had found all the fun there was to be had in baseball, he was proved wrong when he also began writing about it. Writing about exceptional baseball stories wasn't his aim when he set out to write his first book, but he uncovered so many fascinating stories through his research that he found a second book unfurling before his eyes.

Roy's drive for helping others overcome their setbacks and achieve their dreams stems from battling with a setback of his own. His commitment to overcoming this and getting his mind back in the game saw him break down the elements of how to achieve success in baseball, and he's now passionate about sharing everything he's learned with others.

In *The Baseball Player's Guide to Hitting Like a Pro*, you'll find **a clear guide to improving your hitting technique** without focusing on mechanics alone. You'll discover:

- **The 7 key elements needed to build a strong foundation for good hitting**
- Exactly what you can learn from MLB heroes like *Pete Rose* and *Joe Morgan*
- Why bench-time may not be such a bad thing -- and how you can use it to your advantage

- How to look beyond the field to improve your attitude (and why you should)
- The reason why it isn't just top hitters you should be learning from -- and who you should be looking at instead
- **Swing fundamentals broken down into key elements** -- so you know exactly what it is you should be working on
- How to make technique changes that don't ruin improvements you've already made to your swing
- Why confidence is just as problematic as self-doubt -- and what you can do to mitigate it if you're on a streak
- The power of 'Situational Spirit' -- what it is, and how to harness its power
- **A clear path out of your slump so you can start ranking again**

And much more.

Available on Amazon.com

INTRODUCTION

Baseball is a sport of legends. For fans, drama and strategy hang on every pitch. Two teams face each other in a grueling marathon that spans 162 games where only one can come out on top. The players and coaches are involved in a battle that may start with physical talents, but very much involves psychological and emotional aspects that draw fans in with its complexity and competition.

Early in its history, George Herman "Babe" Ruth became one of the first true international celebrities due to the prowess of his play, but also because of his larger-than-life personality and the particular time in history that he was in the limelight. The world was looking for a hero. Even with his records being slowly eclipsed in the modern day, Ruth is still remembered as the face of baseball—the one who elevated the status of the game. He brought baseball and its rich history along with him and helped turn it into a glamorous pastime. He was one of the five inaugural Hall of Fame members. In that Hall, warriors from the field are enshrined in perpetuity with stories that rival those of courageous heroes of ancient battles—their memory is emblazoned upon the fans of the game.

Celebrating that richness are stories of courage, overcoming adversity, hope for the underdog, as well as tragedy and failure. In this book, we look at more than twenty-five stories of men who took the field and played a game to the joy of millions of fans. Arguments often occur between fans as to which player is the best, using statistics and the play that occurs on the field. *A Game of Extremes* attempts to reach beyond that boundary of baseball being just a "game of inches" to look deeper at the special moments created by the heroes, situations, and drama of the game.

"A ballplayer spends a good piece of his life gripping a baseball, and in the end it turns out that it was the other way around all the time."

— JIM BOUTON

1

THE 168 MPH FASTBALL

Baseball has its share of myth and legend. People, to this day, argue whether Babe Ruth called his home run in Game 3 of the 1932 World Series by seemingly pointing to the fence before lifting a ball over it with his next swing. The shot gave the Yankees the lead in the game. They went on to win that game and the World Series. It was the Babe's last time in the fall classic and that moment of the "called shot" left an indelible mark on the history of the game. Ruth, himself, encouraged the claim by providing a voice-over for a newsreel where he says he pointed toward the fence and it was later confirmed by Lou Gehrig.[1] There is a point where much of myth and legend is based on fact, even if it is exaggerated.

Stories that we hear can be like a game of telephone,[2] where a message gets passed down a line of players and comes out the other end. The truth may be a lot different than the stories you hear.

One curious baseball story emerged in *Sports Illustrated*, released in late March for the April 1985 issue of the magazine, showcasing a baseball protégé that the New York Mets had signed. The prospect was a yoga master from Tibet who had the unprecedented ability to throw a baseball as fast as 168 mph with pinpoint accuracy. After the article was released, Mets' players were interviewed on major news stations corroborating the story and taking pictures of the locker that awaited his arrival between George Foster and Daryl Strawberry. The team's fans were overjoyed with the news and amazed at their good luck in finding such a rare star. They looked forward to the rookie taking the field to amass a string of victories where the opposing team barely had a chance to see the ball before it was by them.

On April 2, the Mets held a press conference in which they gave the sad news to fans that Sidd Finch, who obviously had an amazing career ahead of him, had decided to pursue his love of playing the French horn instead of baseball. On April 15, the details of the hoax were officially announced. There was no Sidd Finch.

The whole Mets' organization had played along with the April Fool's joke—the official publication date of the magazine was indeed April 1. Despite the numerous absurdities in the article (he threw with one foot in a work boot and the other bare), no one saw through the hoax. The player who threw with unbelievable accuracy and speed was a complete fabrication played as an elaborate prank on the readers of the magazine. Because it was a respectable resource and long-standing sports publication, readers had no reason to question the story.

The stranger part of the story of Sidd Finch is that not everything about him can be considered a complete fabrication. His name, of course, was made up, as was his existence in reality as a pitcher; but, like all good stories, the myth has some basis in fact.

The October 1970 edition of *Sports Illustrated* had a story about a player who was touted by the coaches and players around him as the fastest flamethrower to ever take the field. Steve Dalkowski spent most of his professional pitching career in the minor league system of the Baltimore Orioles from 1957 to 1965.

Earl Weaver had the chance to manage him in the minor leagues. Weaver said definitively that Dalkowski was clearly faster than Nolan Ryan. There is a rumor that Ted Williams once stepped in the batter's box against him, saw one pitch. and said Dalkowski was the fastest pitcher he'd ever faced and he'd be damned if he ever stood in against him again.

Many players, coaches, and announcers have memories of facing or watching Dalkowski deliver the ball.

"Grab your helmets, run behind buildings, because this guy throws unguided missiles and [even] he doesn't know where they're going."

— LOU BROCK

Part of the problem with Dalkowski's speed was that—unlike Sidd Finch—he lacked the pinpoint control that Finch was said to have. Over 956 innings in the minor leagues Dalkowski amassed an incredible 1,324 strike-outs, an average of 12.5 Ks per nine innings. That rivals the greatest strikeout pitchers of all time. The bigger problem was that he also walked 1,236 batters over that same number of innings and roughly twice as many batters as were able to get a hit off of him. It meant he almost always had at least one man on base.

Several things besides merely the speed contributed to Dalkowski's seeming inability to control where the ball went once it left his hand. Earl Weaver had Dalkowski's intelligence tested, but it is hard to say whether the score reflected his actual intelligence or that his inability to focus gave him no chance to do any better on the test. Weaver did recognize that Dalkowski would lose focus not only between innings or pitches but also as he was throwing the ball. As a means to keep Dalkowski focused, Weaver would take a bucket and bang on it to get his pitcher's head back in the game. Another contributing factor to Dalkowski's wildness may have had something to do with his propensity to drink to excess, even on the nights before ball games. Dalkowski admitted it may have had something to do with the downfall of his career.

But even with testaments from Weaver, Williams, and Brock, Dalkowski was never officially clocked on a radar gun. Using radar to measure pitches didn't come into vogue until the mid-'70s. Before that time it was a matter of relying on word of mouth, myth, and legend.

Cal Ripken Sr., father of the Hall of Famer Cal Ripken Jr., was a respected baseball man, coach, and minor-league catcher. Ripken Sr.'s playing time overlapped with Dalkowski's in the Orioles' farm system. He had the opportunity to catch Dalkowski along with other Oriole greats in the minor leagues such as Jim Palmer and Steve Barber. Ripken Sr. got to know him well enough to have respect for the velocity that was coming at him.

"If you... put [him] on a radar gun today, I think that you'd probably see where Dalkowski threw the ball maybe 110, maybe 115 miles an hour."[3]

— CAL RIPKEN SR.

Dalko was said to be the inspiration for Nuke LaLoosh in the movie *Bull Durham*, as well. LaLoosh was a hard and wild pitcher who lacked control of the ball. It is interesting that a minor league pitcher like Dalkowski would be used, not only as a character in a movie but also as inspiration for one of the biggest pranks in baseball history. It is strange that no one ever thought to turn a camera on Dalkowski to capture his motion just to study it and figure out what he was doing. Still, Dalkowski reigns as the inspiration for Sidd Finch and they both hold a seat, if not in Cooperstown,[4] in the annals of baseball lore.

---

1. In an audio clip from an October 6, 1932 episode of "The Fleischmann's Yeast Hour," Lou Gehrig confirmed the called shot.

2. Generally thought of a children's game, it demonstrates how a message can get scrambled when passing it from one person to the next in a line.

3. *Far From Home—The Steve Dalkowski Story*. https://youtu.be/Kzh42wir_Ms

4. The location of the Baseball Hall of Fame in New York State, USA.

2

HOME RUNS WERE NO FUN

The ongoing power surge in baseball, counted as the number of home runs per year, is attributed to a lot of things. Some say the surge is happening because the players are better trained to hit a long ball. Some claim the ball is being progressively juiced. Some say that the speed pitchers now throw at contributes to the speed of the ball off the bat. Some opt for more obvious factors, like the fact that the season was extended[1] or that there are simply more teams and more players on the field.[2] In all, 2019 saw the greatest number of long balls coming in at 6,776—1,191 more than the previous year. It seems obvious that more than one factor is at play as there were no changes in the number of teams or games.

Changes seem to be adopted to thrill the fans who like to see home runs. But there was one familiar old-timer who didn't often agree with fans—or practically anyone else. He didn't much like losing and was responsible for creating chaos on the base paths. He spiked other players, fought with his own teammates, with umpires, and the police, and is rumored to have killed a man. In 1912, at a game where Detroit was playing the New York Highlanders, he rushed the stands to pummel a fan for shouting insults. But make sure you keep this in mind: Ty Cobb was so famous in his time that a lot of the things he was blamed for were actually done by other people. Some things that were said about Cobb were exaggeration or even pure fiction.[3]

The game of baseball was something Ty Cobb played with an intensity that has rarely been matched in modern-day ball. And although he played life just as hard, not all of his achievements or contempt are accurate depictions of the real man.

It is easy to create a myth when there is nothing to verify it. However, when you go by statistics that are verified by multiple reliable sources, it seems much harder to go wrong. Cobb has one achievement that is in one way or another indelible as it sits as one of many of his triumphs in the record books.

Cobb was not very happy with the new direction the game of baseball had taken since Babe Ruth came on the scene. As Cobb watched Ruth take batting practice once, he reportedly remarked:

"The old game is gone. I guess more people would rather see Babe hit one over the fence than see me steal second. I feel bad about it, for it isn't the game I like to see or play... A lot of these kids, in place of learning the true science of hitting or base running, are trying to knock every pitch over the fence."[4]

— TY COBB

The rumor that emerged from this quote was born as Cobb was sitting with a reporter before a game on May 5, 1925. Perhaps prompted for a response by the reporter, Cobb said: "I'll show you something today. I'm going for home runs for the first time in my career."[5] It seemed as if Cobb suggested that he could just flip a switch and turn on his power to crank the ball over the wall. He just didn't think home runs were as exciting as really playing the game. Here he was, already 38 years old, known more for his unparalleled batsmanship, and suddenly he declared he could become a power hitter at will.

Although the name of the reporter was not revealed beyond the note in Cobb's biography, it is hard to argue with the box scores. That day, on May 5, with his Detroit Tigers mired in a 4–14 slump, Cobb had one of the most memorable offensive games in the history of baseball. He went 6-for-6 with three home runs, a double, and two singles. But that was not the last of it. In the following game on May 6, he went 3-for-6, collecting two more home runs and raising his season batting average to .526 in the process. Cobb went out and clubbed five home runs in two days, something the "Sultan of Swat"[6] never did in his career. It seemed to make the statement that if all fans wanted was home runs, Cobb could hit them practically at will, but the game wasn't going to be as much fun. To say whether that was strictly fun for himself or the fans would be conjecture.

In all, during the 1925 season, Cobb hit a total of only twelve home runs. That is only seven more over the other 138 games he played in that season and none were multi-homer games. It seems such a coincidence that he hit the bulk of his home runs in a period of two games. About 40 percent of the home runs he hit in his career were inside-the-ballpark. Every one of the five home runs hit over those two days went over the fence. It could simply be that he wanted to single-handedly raise his team out of its slump or live up to his boastful prediction. All you have to do is look up the box scores from the games to confirm that it happened, and the boast clearly seems in line with his result.

---

1. From 1904 to 1960 (AL) and 1961 (NL), teams played 154 games. Both added expansion teams and increased the season to 162 games.
2. There has been an ongoing expansion in the number of franchises since the beginning of baseball history. The last expansion, from twenty-eight to thirty teams, was in 1998. The American League expanded to fourteen teams in 1977, and the National League followed sixteen years later in 1993.
3. Cobb's biography by Al Stump was released almost immediately after his death and researchers say that it contains many fallacies.
4. Grantland Rice quoting Cobb in Rice's 1954 autobiography *The Tumult and the Shouting.*
5. Cited in Charles C. Alexander's biography of Cobb, *Ty Cobb.*
6. Another Babe Ruth nickname. There are many.

3

DON'T LOOK BACK, SOMETHING MIGHT BE GAINING ON YOU

Many players throughout the history of the game have had long careers. Most of these players started their pro careers at early ages and not all of them were stars. Others, perhaps, were not ready to give up the game simply for the love of it.

The fact that aging normally affects performance would make you think that anyone who started a career in their 30s was destined to be a short-lived prospect. But a prospect breaking in as a rookie at the age of 42 would certainly be a relic waiting to be put on the shelf. After all, most players retire before they are 40.

Leroy Robert "Satchel" Paige was a truly unique character. In a career that spanned from 1927 in the Negro leagues to his debut as an MLB player in 1948, and into his final appearance in 1965, Paige stayed in the game for as long as anyone.[1] In his final appearance at the age of 59, Paige sat in the bullpen in a rocking chair being served coffee by his nurse. The running joke was that no one really knew how old he was. In that last start for the Kansas City Athletics, Paige went three scoreless innings giving up just one hit to the Boston Red Sox icon Carl Yastrzemski.

"Age is a case of mind over matter. If you don't mind, it don't matter."

— SATCHEL PAIGE

Part of Paige's longevity was his showmanship which made his appearances extravagant and exaggerated like the antics of a circus performer. He attracted crowds for barnstorming games[2] that filled stadiums around the US as they traveled from place to place playing teams in non-league scrimmages.

His windmill windups were a flurry of arms and legs that ended with his high leg kick and delivery. But, from pitch to pitch he varied his arm angles, sometimes hesitating at various points in his delivery. He might windmill three times on one pitch and not the next to sneak in a quick pitch. At times he'd come set with his hands above his head and just freeze. In his stride forward he would sometimes land hard and delay his forward arm movement. It's been reported that he'd even bear down like he was coming with a fastball and just hold the ball as it wrapped around his back and float it in toward the plate. He always had the ability to throw hard and put the ball where he wanted just about every time.

He used these antics in his delivery to intentionally throw off a batter's timing. His windup was practically the opposite of the monotonous, consistent mechanics that is drilled into the head of modern-day pitchers who are taught efficiency and simplify every step of their motion to get the ball where they want it to go. Paige's delivery was anything but simple and efficient. His hesitation pitch[3] became somewhat notorious as being so unconventional that players and coaches thought it must have been illegal. When brought to the attention of American League President Will Harridge, he declared that the hesitation pitch would be charged as a balk. As a balk could only hurt with runners on base, Paige continued with his antics and deceptive deliveries.

"I never threw an illegal pitch. The trouble is, once in a while I toss one that ain't never been seen by this generation."

— SATCHEL PAIGE

Ted Williams faced Paige once, only managing a .222 batting average in 11 at-bats, frustrating the batting master. The great hitter found the pitcher's unconventional approach confounding and could recall the one time that Paige struck him out. After Paige got two strikes on Williams, Williams watched carefully to try to pick up what was coming on the next pitch. As Paige started into a double windup, he lifted his hands up behind his head where Williams (and everyone else in the ballpark) could see them and turned his wrist tipping off that the next pitch was going to be his curveball. Williams got ready to swing at the curve and a fraction of a second later couldn't turn on the ball when Paige uncorked a fastball. Paige being the ultimately confident showman said to Williams: "You ought to know better than to guess with ol' Satch."

Paige's trickery was something he developed using a creative mind and his extensive experience. Success with his deliveries only led to more experiments and tools to add to his articles of deception. According to Paige, he probably pitched over 2,500 games in his career and won 2,000 of them. The claim is really impossible to verify because of the number of years he played, suspect record keeping in some leagues (when records were even kept), and the fact that not every appearance he made was scheduled. He played baseball like a rogue and a vagabond, filling in holes in his contracts and schedule by playing in other leagues and barnstorming. He never considered resting his arm to be important like they do in modern times.

"I sure get [my] laughs when I see in the papers where some major league pitcher says he gets a sore arm because he's overworked, and he pitches every four days. Man, that'd be a vacation for me."

— SATCHEL PAIGE

This mild-mannered clown, showman, craftsman, and magician of the pitching mound was a philosopher as well. The length of his career, long bus rides, and the time he spent in reform school[4] allowed him to be introspective. He used the time to learn about pitching and about himself. While some youths might consider that time as stolen from their childhood, Paige believed it was responsible for his success.

"I traded five years of freedom to learn how to pitch. At least I started my real learning on the Mount.[5] They were not wasted years at all. It made a real man out of me."

— SATCHEL PAIGE

His confidence showed on the mound. It is widely rumored that during games in the Negro leagues, Paige would sometimes call in his outfielders to have a rest and get ready to hit while he finished off the opposing team on his own. While that is easier to believe for a single inning of a regular-season game, Paige's favorite recollection was of a Negro league World Series game in 1942.

According to Paige in his autobiography,[6] he came into Game 2 of the series when the Monarchs led the Grays by two runs. Paige got two outs and let up a triple to the Monarchs' lead-off man, Jerry Benjamin. Paige huddled with his manager and decided to load the bases by walking the next two batters to face the most feared bat in all of the Negro leagues: Josh Gibson. Gibson was known as the Black Babe Ruth and later was a Hall of Fame inductee alongside Paige. This could have been a strategic move to create a force at every base, or just for the sake of the show. But Paige had shown good success against Gibson in the past, so it could be that he saw facing him as an advantage. He went on to intentionally walk two batters as planned, and then up stepped Gibson.

Paige taunted Gibson by telling him what he was going to throw and where he was going to target each pitch with phrases like: "this one's gonna be a pea at your knee." Three pitches later, the mighty Gibson had struck out.

Though published in books and well-publicized, that bit of lore was later debunked by researchers.[7] It seems that Paige had merged parts of two stories and gotten them both wrong. He did face Gibson in that series in the seventh with the bases loaded and two out. After the first batter got out, Paige let up a single—a fielder's choice—and then two more singles to load the bases. When Gibson stepped up, it is likely Paige faced him with confidence, but the news reports mention nothing of taunting. However, in another game that season Paige did walk the batter in front of Gibson with a man on second and two out to induce a weak fly ball. As the autobiography was written twenty years after the event, it is easy to see how the showman in Paige preferred the better story to the right one. In any case, he did beat Gibson both times, so in the win and loss column, the difference doesn't matter. In the end, the myth seems so much more like the man.

One of Satchel's claims to greatness was indeed his ability to stay young and experience a superbly long career. His character and charisma are probably part of the reason for his myth and legend. The true test of that is the observation of his fellow teammates and opposing players who attest to his greatness. It is the reason he was the first Negro league inductee to the Hall of Fame.

Paige left behind a set of six simple rules that he said he lived by to enhance his longevity and life-long success. You may find them useful as you journey through life.

Satchel Paige's Six Rules for Staying Young

1. Avoid fried meats, which angry up the blood.
2. If your stomach disputes you, lie down and pacify it with cool thoughts.
3. Keep the juices flowing by jangling around gently as you move.
4. Go very light on vices such as carrying on in society. The social ramble ain't restful.

5. Avoid running at all times.

6. Don't look back, something may be gaining on you.

---

1. Minnie Minoso, Nick Altrock, and Charlie O'Leary also made guest appearances in MLB games in their later 50s. But Paige currently holds the record for being the oldest active player.
2. A form of traveling exhibition game usually with a hand-selected and star studded team.
3. Paige named some of his pitches and the associated deliveries. Most of them were fastballs.
4. He was sentenced to six years in reform school at the age of 12. Various sources report different reasons, but the most popular notion seems to be that it was for petty larceny.
5. Refers to the location of the reform school in Mount Meigs, Alabama.
6. Paige's autobiography is *Maybe I'll Pitch Forever*.
7. The debunk: https://www.baseball-reference.com/bullpen/1942_Negro_World_Series

4

JAKEY, THE SAUERKRAUT-FACED BOOB

In a day where large shepherd hooks were used to drag acts being pummeled with rotting vegetables off the stage, there lived a jakey,[1] sauerkraut-faced boob[2] who aspired to be in vaudeville. While his bawdy and sour jokes often failed to fill the air with applause and laughter from an audience, he achieved some success on the vaudeville circuit and was not alone in a group of baseball players who turned to the stage to fill out their offseason. His antics on the field and his skills as a multi-positional player did win him praise. He played second fiddle to a famous group of players known as the greatest double-play combination in baseball. He was the odd man out playing alongside the infamous Tinker, Evers, and Chance, whose induction into the Hall of Fame by the "Old-Timers' Committee" left some wondering exactly what the criteria were for being enshrined.

Apparently, some purists did not think it only required having someone remember you in a song.

But if fame could come from a song, it might also arise from a player's ability to entertain a crowd. The plethora of stories that follow in Herman "Germany" Schaefer's wake are stacked so high that it was difficult to know if they were true or just another instance where his over-active imagination ran wild. His mind was always tuned to humor, both on and off the field. It ran the gamut of pranks from the simple to the elaborate.

The incorrigible prankster is charged with throwing his own shoes out the window of a train. He thought he was pulling a stunt on a compartment-mate, having mistaken whose shoes were whose as they rode on through the darkness. When it rained on a game that an umpire refused to call, he walked onto the field in a raincoat and galoshes to hint that it might be time to stop play. A similar thought crossed his mind when stars began to peek out of a twilight sky at old Wrigley Field when he appeared on the field in the light of a lantern. Wrigley didn't have lights on the field until August 8, 1988, so he was clearly ahead of his time.

The winning moments for this clown star were when he earned undeniably memorable achievements. One instance was so infamous that a new rule was created in the official rule book. Another was the rival of a famous at-bat by Babe Ruth. A third was so clever that he won his entire team an extra payday.

Schaefer showed how his mind worked on the serious as well as the absurd at the start of the 1907 World Series. Under the rules at the time, players shared in the gate receipts of the first four games. Schaefer, then captain of the Tigers, thought about what might happen in the unlikely scenario of a tie. He brought up the possibility to officials, wanting to know if the players would be entitled to a share of the fifth game. His reasoning was that the rules called for a game to be played over again if the result was a tie due to rainout or darkness. The issue had never come up before as there had never been a tie game in World Series play. Thinking that the odds of a tie were practically nil, the officials agreed with Schaefer. On the following day, the Tigers and Cubs played to a 3–3 tie in front of the largest crowd to watch a game up until that date. Both teams enjoyed the extra share of the gate.

One Ruthian play that has been well-debated is the Babe's called shot. Some believed it turned from myth to legend after Ruth made the claim he called the shot and Lou Gehrig backed him up. But one player called a shot that was never in dispute, and it was the merry Germany Schaefer. He had been sidelined since May 26 of 1906 after injuring his thumb and was relegated to the coaching box where he took the opportunity to entertain the fans. Down to the final out and losing 2 to 1 with a man on first. The Tiger's pitcher was the next one scheduled to bat. Red Donahue was not particularly known for his batting prowess having hit a mighty .123 that season, so the Tigers manager called on Schaefer to pinch-hit as the White Sox fans began filing out of the stadium.

Catcalls and mockery rained down on Schaefer who had been taunting the crowd himself from the coach's box all game. Before stepping into the batter's box Schaefer turned to the crowd and, according to teammate Davy Jones, he bellowed in his best theatrical voice:

"Ladies and gentlemen, you are now looking at Herman Schaefer, better known as "Herman the Great," acknowledged by one and all to be the greatest pinch-hitter in the world. I am now going to hit the ball into the left-field bleachers. Thank you."[3]

— GERMANY SCHAEFER

Although it seemed completely unlikely for a player who hit a total of nine home runs in his fifteen-year career, Schaefer promptly sent the first pitch over the left-field wall. As he rounded the bases Schaefer called his progress around the diamond like a horse race. He slid into each bag hamming it up in a way that probably would have gotten the opposing team to do some head-hunting in his next at-bat in the modern day. As he crossed home he slid in, leaped to his feet, and shouted "Schaefer wins by a nose!" and then kindly thanked his audience for their attention. The homer had put the Tigers ahead and they stayed there to the great dismay of the Sox fans who had returned to their seats. Although this was the only home run Schaefer called, it is said that he called other hits during his career. He was said to often be wrong, but accuracy isn't anything if you are a legend for getting one right.

"Nobody remembers those times, they only remember when you're right."[4]

— DAVE NIEHAUS

His antics were indeed admirable on and off the field, but the one play he instigated that was cause for a change in the rule book is probably the best known. It was August 4, 1911—the first game of a double-header. Schaefer became one of the few professional baseball players to ever be recognized for stealing first base. Sort of. According to the box score, he was only credited with one steal in that game; it must have been great confusion for everyone involved, including the official scorer.

With the score tied 0–0 in the bottom of the ninth and two out, Schaefer was on first and Clyde Milan on third. Schaefer broke for second hoping to draw a throw from the White Sox catcher, but Fred Payne did not take the bait. With the winning run on third, there was no reason to try and nab Schaefer at second. Having failed to draw a throw, Schaefer apparently called out to Milan saying they should try it again. On the next pitch, Schaefer broke for first, again disappointed not to have drawn a throw.

The White Sox manager came out to complain about the shenanigans on the base paths and as the manager was arguing with the umpire, Schaefer broke for second again. This time he drew a throw and got into the rundown he was looking for. Milan took advantage of the confusion and the rundown but was tagged out on the throw to the plate and the game went into extra innings.[5] A lesson to be learned is that if it is not specifically disallowed in the rule book, it is an option during play.

Herman "Germany" Schaefer permanently left his mark on the game as the legend who stole first base with what was officially known as Rule 52, Section 2, which states:

"Any runner is out when... after he has acquired legal possession of a base, he runs the bases in reverse order for the purpose of confusing the defense or making a travesty of the game."[6]

— OFFICIAL BASEBALL RULES

---

1. At the turn of the twentieth century, this was a term used to describe a chronic alcoholic. "Jake" refers specifically to methylated spirits.

2. The unfortunate subject of this story suffered from smallpox scarring, and he was often called a "sauerkraut-faced boob" by hecklers.

3. Lawrence Ritter, *The Glory of Their Times*.

4. Hall of Fame baseball announcer.

5. Various accounts of the story differ. Some claim Schaefer pulled the stunt more than once. Supposedly, the first time was May 30, 1907, when Detroit was playing at Cleveland and it was successful. Schaefer was credited for a stolen base in both the 1907 and 1911 games, and both were 1 to 0 games that went into extra innings, so if the play occurred in the bottom of the ninth it failed both times. Further problems arise in the story claiming the play was a success is that Schaefer's team lost in 1907 and won in 1911. If the play was successful in 1907 Schaefer's team would have won; if the play was successful in 1911, it would have had to occur in the eleventh inning. No other player on Schaefer's team was credited with a steal on those dates, so a successful outcome is likely a stretch of reality. Milan did score the winning run in 1911, it just was not likely via a stolen base unless the official scorer did not give Milan a stolen base because of an error on the play. The version used here most closely resembles what was also recounted in both the *Washington Post* and the *Chicago Tribune*.

6. Rule 5.09(b)(10) of the Official Baseball Rules: http://mlb.mlb.com/mlb/official_info/official_rules/foreword.jsp

5

TEN TONS OF GUACAMOLE AND A SAMURAI SWORD

Some baseball players are odd because they try to be. Others are just naturally gifted in the art of eccentricity. Players don't have to be from the early 1900s to claim the right to peculiar notions and colorful personalities. Maybe when you are a star and you play a game in front of a camera where your every word has a chance to come off with a twist, you have more opportunity to seem different. Or maybe you just are.

In 2004, a player who would later go on to win six Gold Gloves, play in the All-Star game six times, earn two Silver Slugger awards, a Cy Young, and win the ERA title twice was called into the Kansas City Royals office at their Triple-A affiliate. The 20-year-old was informed that they were sending him to the big league club—the dream of every minor league player was just dropped in his lap. The young player paused a moment contemplating the news and then said to his manager:

"I don't know. Do you think if we asked them, they would let me go back to Single-A and be a shortstop? I think I can be a pretty good shortstop."

— ZACK GREINKE

The idea took his manager aback. It would not be the strangest thing Greinke said or did in the career that has him edging close to the Hall of Fame as a pitcher. His manager encouraged him to take the opportunity.

It seemed Greinke wanted what he had in high school: a chance to play every day and keep himself occupied. In his own words, he doesn't think hitting is that hard. He was, after all, a .400 hitter in high school and had only turned into a pitcher in his senior year. That's when he started turning heads with his arm to the tune of a 0.55 ERA in sixty-three innings with 118 Ks.

The Royals took him sixth overall in the draft as a pitcher who had only logged those sixty-three innings.

Instead of playing all the time, he was filled with doubts about his career choice. Along with that grew a latent and crippling anxiety that came on him so badly that he considered quitting the game for good. He didn't want to be around people anymore and preferred being in nature.

"I was going to get a job where I didn't have to be around people all the time. Mainly, just mowing grass was my goal."

— ZACK GREINKE

It turned out Greinke was suffering from social anxiety disorder. Some people with the condition go a lifetime without being diagnosed or treated. Even things that were once a great joy are no longer stimulating for those with the condition. The fear it can bring on is crippling, and it nearly ended his career. His managers saw that something was wrong. They sent him home to seek treatment and after treatment he was able to rekindle his love for the game. Then he set about becoming the best player he could be. Like in everything else, he adopted a burning sense of competition, became a student of pitching, and developed his talents.

He seems to have settled back into his body in a way that lets his personality flourish.

He grew into a player that people think can do just about anything he wants to with a baseball. He can tell batters what is coming and they still can't handle what he throws. He is a player who has already made over $300 million dollars in his career, and it was because he came back with hope.

"Hope is a good thing, maybe the best of things, and no good thing ever dies." [1]

— ANDY, *SHAWSHANK REDEMPTION*

Some think that Greinke has become as famous for his quirks as for his play. Before signing a record-breaking contract with Arizona for $206 million over six years—an average of a little over $34 million a year—the curious things were the reported riders. The team and Greinke's agent haggled for weeks over the terms before hammering them out in one day. It made no sense to Greinke why they couldn't just go in a room and get it done the first time. The complications may have to do with how unusual the rider requests were. The contract reportedly includes the following:

- Ten tons of free, high-quality guacamole
- Minority stake in one Chipotle franchise
- *The Shawshank Redemption* on Blu-Ray
- At least five games per year as a position player
- Samurai swords[2]

These are the kinds of demands that an event organizer might expect from a rock star. Perhaps in a way he has become one to the fans who love the way he plays the game. His response, when asked about the restaurant and guacamole, made Greinkian sense. He was upset that they had raised the prices $0.30 on the menu item from $1.50 so that the guacamole which he already thought was overpriced now set him back $1.80. Never mind trying to tell him about the millions he is making. Even with pricing food on menus, Greinke needs to compete.

"I don't really love the guacamole... It's not about the guacamole itself, I just don't want to let them win."

— ZACK GREINKE

It may confuse some people to follow the curvy lines of logic. For example, winning the Cy Young may have played a part in Greinke's request for samurai swords. When he received the actual award, he wasn't as impressed as he was with the gift Mizuno gave him. He gave the award to his parents, as he had always done with his awards.

"I've only kept one award in my whole life, and it's the coolest thing ever. Mizuno gave me a samurai sword for winning the Cy Young. It's awesome... It's got a hanger thing and every-thing. I'm going to hang it up and, maybe, start a collection. Not a gun collection, but a samurai sword collection."

— ZACK GREINKE

Greinke is a very giving guy. He shares his trophies like he shares his knowledge with other players, especially when he thinks he can help his team. Once, when rookie Alex Gordon was having trouble at the plate, Greinke offered to help the youngster out. Gordon accepted the offer. Greinke was a pitcher, but he had to know something about hitting. Didn't he?

They went off to the video room where Gordon expected Greinke to reveal a great secret that would get him out of his funk. Greinke popped in a favorite video of his fourth at-bat in the major leagues. During that at-bat, he hit his first MLB home run. He played it for Gordon several times without saying anything then he said: "Do more of that."

"I don't want to name names, but there were guys I played with that were so stupid that they're really good, because their mind never gets in the way."

— ZACK GREINKE

In a way, that may seem like a session that would have done Gordon absolutely no good. But maybe it was Greinke's own unique way of communicating to Gordon that he was over-thinking at the plate. It seems you can never tell with Greinke.

---

1. One of Zack Greinke's favorite films.
2. Taken from an official announcement by Major League Baseball: https://www.mlb.com/cut4/zack-greinke-signs-with-arizona-diamondbacks/c-158874402

6

THE STEAK AND POTATO OF RETIRED NUMBERS

A ce Bailey was a hockey player who doesn't belong in a book on baseball. That is except for one unprecedented achievement. He was the first professional sports player to have his number retired (number 6). Retiring a number has since become the ideal way to honor a player. It may be for their contributions and achievements as a player, sometimes as a marker of a career cut tragically short, and usually stands as a symbol of respect, pride, and emotion. Usually.

The first number ever retired in baseball was number 4, belonging to baseball's Iron Horse. Lou Gehrig played 2,130 straight games before taking himself out of the Yankees lineup as he felt his capabilities as a player had diminished too much to continue to play. The date that his number was retired, July 4, 1939, is one that any true baseball fan remembers as the day the fading star gave his speech.

"Today, I consider myself the luckiest man on the face of the earth... I might have been given a bad break, but I've got an awful lot to live for"

— LOU GEHRIG

The day was an emotional outpouring for a great star and competitor that happened to fall under the shadow of Babe Ruth but rose to his own immortality in the sport.

This chapter could well be full of great heroes, and here we find Dave Bresnahan. This career minor leaguer was a backup catcher with a minuscule batting average, but he managed to have his number, 59, retired by the Williamsport Bills in 1987. The Bills were Cleveland's Double-A farm team, and four retired numbers hang on the outfield fence at Bowman Field. You might think this is a lackluster background for a player to achieve the honor of having his number retired. It does seem that way.

Maybe it had something to do with his baseball heritage, which is significant. His great-uncle Roger Bresnahan was a Hall of Famer who had a long playing and managerial career. Also a catcher, he worked behind the plate as battery mate to Christy Mathewson[1] and was the first catcher inducted to the Hall. He was instrumental in incorporating shin guards and batting helmets into the game as an innovator in player protection. But, certainly pedigree isn't enough to see your number retired.

Here is how it happened.

In the second game of a double-header on August 31 in 1987 against the Reading Phillies, Bresnahan had the opportunity to play in a game rather than warm his usual spot on the bench. In the fifth inning, the opposing team had a player reach second with only one out. For some reason, Bresnahan was calling breaking balls and change-ups as if to induce a ground ball to the right side of the infield. Not a typical strategy if you want to win a game by keeping the runners from advancing. But, with only a few weeks to play and the Bills some twenty-eight games out without a chance to get back in the race, winning wasn't the only thing on Bresnahan's mind.

After successfully helping the other team advance their runner to third, Bresnahan called a time out for an equipment malfunction. He claimed that his mitt was damaged and he needed to get his backup from the dugout. He trotted off the field and returned a moment later and got in his crouch. He called a slider low and away off the plate and tried to pick the runner off third as he had against the same team a few games ago. Even though the throw was good, it somehow got by the third baseman and went on into left field. The runner on third, thinking that the ball had gotten away, started to dash toward home.

Bresnahan stepped up to the runner flying in from third and reached out to tag him before he reached the plate. He revealed the ball in his glove to the runner and the umpire and started to make his way off the field having manufactured the last out of the inning.

Lots of confusion emerged at that moment. The third-base umpire went into the outfield and retrieved what he knew went flying by him. He lifted it up and yelled out: "It's a [expletive] potato!" Bresnahan had schemed to carve a potato to look like a baseball and fool everyone on the field—except his teammates, who already knew about the gag.

The umpire behind the plate was being evaluated that day by a supervisor in the stands, and he was pretty unhappy to have a situation where he had to make a call that wasn't in the rule book. He was sure the section on deceptively substituting a ball with a potato was missing. However, Rule 8.01 (c) covers pretty much every other instance not already accounted for in the rule book:

"Each umpire has authority to rule on any point not specifically covered in these rules."

The umpire made his decision and chose to let the runner score. Bresnahan's manager pulled him from the game immediately and fined him $50. The next day the team released him and he never played another game in pro ball. With his release, Bresnahan saw no reason to pay the fine to a team for who he no longer played. Instead, he bought two sacks of potatoes, dumped them on his former manager's desk, and left behind a note.

"Of course you don't expect me to pay the $50 fine, but here's at least 50 potatoes. This spud's for you."

— DAVE BRESNAHAN

While the current management was pretty distressed with his behavior, the team's new General Manager, Rick Muntean had a very different view. The Williamsport Bills held "Dave Bresnahan Potato Night" in 1988 where the play was reenacted and Dave's number was retired in front of 2,734 fans who each paid $1 and a potato to get in. It was the second-highest attendance of the season.

"Baseball purists ask why he made a travesty of the game. But we think Dave did something that is the essence of baseball—he had fun with it. At a time when the business of baseball dominates the headlines, he brought baseball back to the field."

— RICK MUNTEAN

The saddest part of this story is the true history of spud substitution. It could be that Dave Bresnahan thought he was being unique, but he himself may have heard hand-me-down stories from his great-uncle about players who had pulled off spud tricks long before. There is a story from the *Dallas Morning News* in 1895 (coincidentally in Williamsport) that reports of a potato being put in play in a game between the Williamsporters and Lock Haven by a pitcher who duped a runner at first base into trying to take second by throwing a spud wide of first on a pick-off. The ump called the player out, but the Williamsporters protested the play and the game ended.[2]

In 1889, a player on the Staten Island Athletic Club attempted a similar play in a game against Yale. The runner was successfully put out, but the player was asked to resign from the Athletic Club.[3] Umpire Bill Klem called it "an old gag." Regardless of the age of the prank, in a D-League Lafayette White Sox game in 1934, a catcher did the same exact maneuver as Bresnahan, throwing the "ball" over the third baseman's head, then tagging out the runner with the real ball he had in his glove.[4]

Regardless if he was aware of the play from stories handed down through the pedigree of generations, Bresnahan is the man who was honored by having his number retired for just one play in his otherwise lackluster career. His own words close the story well.

"Lou Gehrig had to play in 2,130 consecutive games and hit .340 for his number to be retired, and all I had to do was bat .140 and throw a potato."

— DAVE BRESNAHAN

1. Hall of Famer, considered one of the best pitchers of all time.
2. Peter Morris, *A Game of Inches: The Stories behind the Innovations That Shaped Baseball.*
3. H. Allen Smith and Ira L. Smith, *Low and Inside.*
4. Also from the book by Peter Morris.

7

LEGEND OF SURPRISE WITH DOMINANCE

The record for most consecutive batters hit by a pitch is three. One pitcher did it within his eleven-pitch start on May 1, 1974, in the first five pitches of the game. In fact, he almost hit Pete Rose with the last warm-up pitch as he stood looking on from outside the batter's box. It took two pitches to hit Pete Rose, one to hit Joe Morgan, and two more to hit Dan Driessen. He followed that with a four-pitch walk to Tony Perez which found Perez dodging balls all aimed at him. The walk knocked in a run and put the Reds in the lead. When Johnny Bench came up, he dodged two pitches thrown close to his head.

Danny Murtaugh, manager of the Pittsburgh Pirates, came out to talk to his pitcher and when he had no excuse for being so wild, decided to take him out of the game.

Now that might be the type of performance you might expect if a pitcher was extremely impaired or suddenly found himself with the yips. Eleven pitches to five batters, none of them strikes, and apparently, the pitcher was unable to control where the ball was going —except that it kept going directly at the hitters. It seems especially true that the performance was unusual for a pitcher who normally showed good control.

Such a poor performance might be what you would have expected to happen for a player when he was high or drunk and then went out and pitched a game anyway. In reality, the pitcher Murtaugh removed from the game had vowed that he would hit as many Reds in his May 4 start as possible days before he took the field. He looked at the Reds as the arch enemies of the Pirates, and he wanted to show them who was boss.

"I've pitched some good games at Cincinnati, but the majority I've lost, because I feel like we weren't aggressive... We gonna get down. We gonna do the do. I'm going to hit these mother-fuckers."[1]

— DOCK ELLIS

Dock had simply gone out to knock down the opposing batters one after the next to put the fear back into the games they had against the Reds. It was a plan he put in place and his control was practically impeccable. It just wasn't accurate according to the typical rules of balls and strikes. The performance was to the score of Ellis' own concerto.

Let's say you take this same pitcher and put him on the mound when he is actually impaired and high on LSD and Benzedrine. It seems impossible that a pitcher could navigate through the effects of hallucinogenics and speed while pitching a game. But that's just what Ellis did on July 12, 1970.

By his own admission, he never took the field without being high. He also claimed that the majority of players in the league took the field with some level of Dexamyl in their system. It was the stimulant of choice in those days, used as a performance enhancer.

"I was so used to medicating myself. That's the way I was dealing with the feeling of failure. I pitched every game in the major leagues under the influence of drugs... It was just a part of the game, you know? You get to themajor leagues and you say 'I got to stay here. What do I need?"

— DOCK ELLIS

The day Dock pitched on LSD and "benzos," started on June 10—two days before his scheduled start. Ellis went to visit a friend in Los Angeles after a game in San Francisco because the team had the next day off. By his account, he dropped some acid at the airport in anticipation that the dose would hit him just when he was where he wanted to be. It is unclear if he partook in other drugs or alcohol over the next day, but that would explain his strange response to his friend's wife on the afternoon of the 12th.[2] Still at his friend's house, his host reminded Ellis he needed to get to the ballpark because he had to pitch that evening. He was sure she was wrong and that it was still the 11th. He had another whole day before he was scheduled, and told her she was crazy. She grabbed the newspaper and brought him the sports page. It seems our hero had lost all track of time. To make matters worse, he had already taken some more acid when he awoke that morning. Being two in the afternoon with game time at six, all he knew was he had better get to the airport.

He arrived ninety minutes before the first pitch and was still quite high from the LSD he had taken that morning. He went to visit a lady in the stands who had a "pretty little gold pouch." She was his golden fairy in the stands who used to always supply him with Benzedrine, another stimulant, when he came to play in San Diego. After he got what he went to see the good fairy for, he downed the pills before he reached the dugout, adding a more typical dose of speed to his lingering acid experience. He started to feel elated from the pills just in time for the team to take the field.

> "[I am sure] the opposing team and my team-
> mates knew I was high but they didn't know
> what I was high on. They had no idea what
> LSD was other than what they see on TV with
> the hippies."
>
> — DOCK ELLIS

Ellis claimed that when the game started that evening there was a fine mist in the air that lasted all through the game. The historic weather report doesn't agree.[3] When he looked where the catcher was supposed to be, Ellis couldn't see the hitters, let alone the signs. All he could tell was if there was a batter on the right or left side of the plate. The catcher put reflective tape on his fingers so Ellis could see the signals.

Whenever he recounted his drug-induced experience to various writers, his consistent memory was that he could only remember bits and pieces of the game. He had a distinct feeling of euphoria. At times he couldn't feel the ball. When he could, the ball was sometimes too small or too large. Sometimes he saw the catcher, and sometimes he didn't. The chewing gum in his mouth felt like it turned into powder. Richard Nixon took over calling balls and strikes as the home plate umpire.

Jimmy Hendricks came to bat holding a guitar to take his turn at the plate.

There were times when the ball was hit back at Ellis and he jumped because he saw it coming at him fast. Every time the catcher threw the ball back it was so big he had to use two hands. One time he had to cover first base on a grounder to the right side and he probably surprised himself by not getting lost on the way. He ran the play perfectly, catching the ball and tagging the base all in one motion. Then he said: "Oooh, I just made a touchdown."

"I didn't pay no attention to the score, you know. I'm trying to get the batters out. I'm throwing a crazy game. I'm hitting people, walking people, throwing balls in the dirt, they're going everywhere."

— DOCK ELLIS

The Pirates had a rookie on the team at that time named Dave Cash. After the first inning Cash teased Ellis saying he had a no-hitter. Around the fourth inning, Cash said it again. The rookie should have known better and sensed, like Ellis did, that the other players wanted Cash to shut up. It's a superstition that you are not supposed to say anything if somebody's throwing a no-hitter.

Ellis finished the wild outing with 8 walks, 6 strikeouts, and one hit batsman; he let up three stolen bases, but even with all those base runners, he didn't let up a run. Willie Stargell commanded all of the offense with 2 solo home runs, and the Pirates won 2 to 0. But that was it. No balks. No wild pitches. Oh, and the Padres didn't manage a hit all game. Ellis pitched his one and only no-no on LSD.

Ellis claims he never used LSD during the baseball season again, but still used amphetamines. He later admitted to regretting being so high that day because it robbed him almost entirely of any memory of his greatest professional performance.

One curious quote by fellow teammate Al Oliver suggests that if Dave Bresnahan deserves his number retired for pegging a potato into left field, Ellis deserves something even greater.

"I know this: if you can pitch a no-hitter on LSD, you should be in Cooperstown."

— AL OLIVER

1. Quoted from two different parts of Donald Hall's, *Dock Ellis in the Country of Baseball.*
2. It is hard to believe that there is a credible report from anyone if Ellis could not remember the entirety of June 11, and he is the one mostly responsible for reporting the story.
3. According to weather history there was no mist or precipitation on the date of the no-hitter. https://www.wunderground.com/history/daily/KPIT/date/1970-7-12

8

BASEBALL'S NAMELESS HEROES AND HYPOCRITES

Mythic heroes sometimes draw attention to themselves by attempting to outperform the gods. The gods then typically throw a hissy-fit and subject the daring heroes to scrutiny because no human can be like a god.

However, heroes still dare to challenge the gods as if they don't know what is coming. The typical hero is endowed with powers lesser than the gods but far greater than typical human abilities. In order to get these powers they turn to PEDs[1] as if they were PEZ.[2]

Heroes have goals. Odysseus[3] battled with the gods and other beasts in order to end up in epic poems and celebrated in songs so that people remembered his name.

The real message is to step up and risk your life so people make movies about you after you are dead.

"*Messenger Boy:* **The Thessalonian you're fighting. He's the biggest man I've ever seen. I wouldn't want to fight him.**

Achilles: **That's why no-one will remember your name.**"

— FROM THE 2004 MOVIE, *TROY*

Greek gods, in particular, can be colossal jerks. Tantalus, a demigod,[4] cooked up his son to serve at his father's dinner party. It was an unusual choice but he was tasked with cooking dinner and, considering the guest list, it would have been bad to screw it up. Maybe Tantalus burned the pig or goat or calf or whatever he was supposed to serve and the only thing handy was the kid. You get hired to cater a party to the gods and you need to step up.

When his daddy, Zeus, found out that his son served everyone "grandson fricassee," Zeus got a little pissed. He punished Tantalus by sending him to Hades for eternity to stand in a pool of water that he couldn't drink, with a fruit tree just out of his reach. The only thing Tantalus did was cook his son to fill his contractual obligation and make daddy's guests happy.

It turns out that the kid getting cooked was no big deal. The gods looked at the stew, got suspicious, found out what happened, and they just took the bits of grandson out of the stew and stuck him all back together as they might do with a jigsaw puzzle. Gods can do that sort of thing. A chunk of arm here, a little liver there, and voila. They resurrected Pelops (the grandson) and he got to hang around with Poseidon, learn how to drive the divine chariot, and he got to sport a really cool shoulder made of ivory. The shoulder had to be replaced because Demeter—some goddess invited to the grandson BBQ—ate the kid's shoulder absentmindedly while crying about losing her daughter. Weep, weep, weep. Apparently, you can't unchew a body part. Consider the replaced shoulder something like Tommy John surgery or bone chip removal.

You may start to see what all this blather about Greek gods being crazy has to do with baseball. Hypocrisy. In Greek mythology, that would be Hippocrates: the god of silence, secrets, and confidentiality. That's where "hypocrisy" comes from. Hypocrites claim to have all these high standards when part of what they "achieve" is keeping their mouths closed.

Unless you are some kind of baseball historian, you may never have heard of James Francis "Pud" Galvin.[5] The guy is in the Hall of Fame.[6] Pud won forty-six games in 1883 and 1884. That is not a total of forty-six games, which would be good enough. It is two years in a row winning forty-six games for a total of ninety-two wins. In each season he threw more than 630 innings. 1,260 innings in two years. That is a career for some Hall of Fame pitchers.[7]

In those two seasons he had more than seventy complete games, with over 140 complete games in two years. He ended his career with 365 wins, a 2.85 ERA, and more than 6,000 innings pitched in fifteen years. That's an average of 400 innings a year. Nolan Ryan, who is considered an iron man for playing baseball for twenty-seven years, came up about 400 innings short of Pud's total.

Just putting up those numbers made Pud a serious stud-muffin. If that kind of endurance and longevity came in a bottle, every player would be drinking it. Time to learn about Brown-Séquard Elixir.[8] The late 1800s were still the age of snake-oil salesmen. People went from town to town selling magic potions to cure what ailed you. This particular elixir was different than a lot of concoctions in that it was developed by an actual doctor through research. It was originally made from the testicles of guinea pigs and dogs and was supposed to prolong life, enhance energy, and preserve youth. How did you take it? By injection. What did you get from it? Testosterone. Testosterone is a PED. Taking PEDs is now illegal in baseball.

If that statement is setting off alarms in your head at the moment, it means that PEDs were being used in baseball at least as early as 1889. This is recognized by Pud's participation in using the elixir before a game where his team, the Pittsburgh Alleghenys, played the Boston Beaneaters on Tuesday, August 13, 1889. The test was practically celebrated by the news.

"[Pud] Galvin was one of the subjects at a test of the Brown-Sequard Elixir at a medical college in Pittsburgh on Monday. If there still be doubting Thomases who concede no virtue of the elixir, they are respectfully referred to Galvin's record in yesterday's Boston-Pittsburgh game. It is the best proof yet furnished of the value of the discovery."

— *THE WASHINGTON POST*, AUGUST 14, 1889

Galvin had openly participated in a test of the elixir. He took a shot in the thigh that contained testosterone. In that game, the day after the shot, Galvin pitched a two-hit shutout, winning 9 to 0, and was unusually successful at the plate hitting a double and a triple to help his own cause. His vitality had been failing since his dominance years before, and it appeared the elixir helped Galvin turn back the clock. He'd been looking for a way to get back to his heyday of '83 and '84 because in '88 and '89 he'd only been able to muster forty-six wins total—twenty-three two years in a row.

Some believe the result was psychosomatic and equivalent to the confidence gained from taking a miracle sugar pill. Galvin, *The Washington Post*, and more than 12,000 physicians who distributed Brown-Sequard's Elixir after the documented test probably believed in the effects. One thing was clear: after the test, everyone wanted to use the elixir, find something like it, or find something even better.

Even in the early 1900s, baseball players turned to cocaine and other substances that are on the current PED list to play to their potential. There were no rules against it. But baseball is not where performance enhancement started. Greek Olympians—the heroes of their time and gods on earth—used performance enhancers.[9]

"The ancient Olympic champions were professionals who competed for huge cash prizes... Most forms of what we would call cheating were perfectly acceptable to them, save for game-fixing. There is evidence that they gorged themselves on meat—not a normal dietary staple of the Greeks—and experimented with herbal medications in an effort to enhance their performances... The ancient Greek athletes also drank wine potions, used hallucinogens, and ate animal hearts or testicles in search of potency."

— SALLY JENKINS, "WINNING, CHEATING HAVE ANCIENT ROOTS," *THE WASHINGTON POST*, AUGUST 3, 2007

It would probably shock most people to know Babe Ruth took a shot of sheep testicle extract to enhance his performance. That he tried at least once suggests that it wasn't the only thing he did as he felt his skills start to decline. It would not be a surprise that soldiers who returned from war in the '40s and '50s—who used amphetamines to counteract fatigue, elevate mood, heighten endurance, and fight for their lives and American values—figured those same drugs might help them on the ball field. What player wouldn't want to heighten alertness and improve their ability to see the ball?

The most important thing that happened to draw attention to PEDs was when a few athletes tried to push the boundaries of how far they could go in taking them. Deaths started happening. The alleged motto of Tommy Simpson, a champion cyclist who died in 1967, was:

"If it takes ten to kill you, take nine and win."[10]

— TOMMY SIMPSON

Simpson made no denials about taking drugs. On the day of his death, during the thirteenth stage of the Tour de France on July 13, 1967, he had amphetamines with him and they were detected in his system.

Even horses were testing positive for banned substances.[11] Surprise steroid testing at the Pan American games in 1983 found nineteen athletes failed testing while two dozen more simply left the competition with no explanation. Let's guess what the reason was for their departure.

The use of PEDs reflects the mindset of high-performing athletes. Winning is everything. Individuals may take almost anything in the belief that it will give them a physical or psychological advantage over their opponents.

Widespread use of "greenies" by major league players for decades before MLB issued a list of banned substances[12] did not put fans or the press in a tizzy. If modern rules were applied to former players, it would remove many of the plaques hanging in the heralded Hall of Fame. No player has ever been removed from the Hall, even after admitting to using drugs that are now considered illegal.

According to Tom House,[13] he remembers how a teammate joked that they didn't lose a game so much as they were "out-milligrammed." In other words, players respected each other's elite talents but may not have been taking the right drugs or enough of them. Rumor has it that when they found out what drug defeated them, they took that too.

Players were prone to taking performance enhancers as a means to level the playing field, maximize their performance, and compete. With advances in science and technology, players had access to more efficient enhancements than hamster balls. There was no official rule change in baseball until 2005,[14] and HGH was not specifically banned until 2011. If you want to create a giant or a god, HGH is the drug you would give to the scrawny kid who gets beat up on the playground. It is known to speed healing and build muscle and bone. That sounds like a benefit in treatment of injuries.

"Shouldn't amphetamines—or 'greenies'— which were widely used in the majors for decades before modern steroids became prevalent, be classified as 'performance-enhancing drugs'? If so, shouldn't we penalize players that came to prominence during the pre-steroids era? When should the guilt-by-association end?"

— ISAAC RAUCH, FILED WITH THE
BASEBALL HALL OF FAME, 2013

In a 2001 interview, when asked how Hall of Fame voters should treat the likes of Bonds and Clemens, Hall president Jeff Idelson referred to the "character clause"—a rule that demands "voting shall be based upon the player's record, playing ability, integrity, sportsmanship, character, and contributions to the team(s) on which the player played." The curious point is whether "integrity" and "character" have changed in meaning with time. But there is also a question as to if a player's "record," "ability," and "contributions to the team" come at the expense of a single element for which no rules were enforced.

Elite players in different eras compiled some of the most ethereal and unbelievable achievements that dwarfed the best in the game and will likely never be approached again. The gods of the game who have achieved the most hits (Pete Rose, 4,256),[15] won seven Cy Young awards (Roger Clemens), the most home runs (Barry Bonds, 762 career; 73 in a season), and may be a descendant of other baseball gods like, say, Willie Mays. Or at least have one as a godfather.[16] Players whose forefathers admitted to using PEDs that are now banned[17] have to suffer their accomplishments being belittled because the rules have changed. All they wanted to do was match the advantages taken by the competition. Their biggest mistake was often to stand out enough to come under the microscope because their "ability," "record," and "contributions to the team(s) on which the player played" were outstanding.

"You can give a [mere mortal] all the PEDs you want, but you still have to make contact."

— SKIP BAYLESS, TALKING ABOUT
BARRY BONDS ON *UNDISPUTED*

You can't hit a baseball without the skill to hit one. A pill does not give you the recognition to be so respected that you are walked with the bases loaded just to avoid the possibility of having you swing a bat.[18] What minimal gain does a player actually get when they stalk a mountain like Tommy Simpson or drop like a fly from heatstroke because of a bad calculation in a dose like Steve Belcher?[19] To them, the greater risk might be not using every advantage available to perform.

The influence of media and the ability to misinform, create sensationalist positions, and distort perception is something looked at broadly in the pages of this book. The cheating starts when a rule is in place. It is dishonorable not to follow it. Rules change with time and they are meant to affect play going forward, not looking back. Originally marijuana use by baseball players was prohibited. Now that laws have changed, players who previously tested positive for recreational use would not be flagged today. Tantalus should have had other reasons not to put his own kid in the oven, but the rule was not established until after there was no way to take it back. He went to hell.

In the years that are to come, players who are committed will find ways to compete. The practices they take on to achieve their edge might be more sophisticated and later come into question. For example, some people think it is criminal to use PEDs although it seems to have been done all throughout the history of baseball. But now players even associated with that era of baseball's indecision end up at fault.[20]

If it is considered unfair to take drugs that enhance performance, where does the line get drawn in the sand? There are other things that enhance performance. Tommy John was 13 and 3 in 1974 before ending his season to have surgery to reconstruct his ulnar collateral ligament. He came back to continue his admirable career and won 288 games with a 3.34 ERA.[21] It doesn't seem quite right that operations get to slide under the radar. Since Tommy John acted as a guinea pig for the surgery, more than 500 MLB players have had the procedure—it is not documented whether each one was needed or not. Even Tommy John spoke out against the surgery being used for performance enhancement.[22] If you look at performance enhancement surgery and compare it to the risks and objections of PEDs, the lists are similar:

- The person having the procedure is taking a risk and can die from the surgery.[23]
- The procedure can be used inappropriately instead of as a means to fix a clearly identifiable problem.[24]
- The procedure is legal.[25]

"Some parents think: 'My son's a pitcher. If we give him Tommy John surgery, he's gonna throw harder. Bull..."

— TOMMY JOHN

It is not enough to condemn performance enhancement without considering its history, reason, definition, and rules. Players who are pressured to perform may not always make the right decision—end up putting their own children in the oven. But it is likely that they never did so without a motivation to be more like the gods.

1. Performance Enhancing Drugs.
2. PEZ is a candy made by an Austrian candy company. The candy became famous more for the collectability of the candy dispensers than the candy itself. The dispenser has a head which gets tipped back to release one candy at a time.
3. All you have to know is this guy was a bad sailor who got lost for ten years trying to get home from a war and gouged out the eye of a cyclops.
4. A child born of procreation between a human and a god.
5. "Pud" stood for "Pudding," because Galvin was said to reduce hitters to pudding at the plate.
6. Elected in 1965 by the Veterans Committee.
7. Mariano Rivera threw just 1,283 innings in his nineteen-year career.
8. Developed by Charles-Édouard Brown-Séquard, a 72-year-old physician seeking a solution to his own decline.
9. The longer history of this is available online: https://sportsanddrugs.procon.org/historical-timeline/ , "History of Performance Enhancing Drugs in Sports."
10. Mr. Simpson is referring specifically to a type of amphetamine he used.
11. Dancer's Image, May 4, 1968 was disqualified from a win at the Kentucky Derby for phenylbutazone. The drug is an NSAID and was later made legal in horse racing.
12. The official updated list: https://en.wikipedia.org/wiki/List_of_banned_substances_in_baseball
13. A pitcher with an eight-year career in the '70s who observed the use of performance enhancing drugs first-hand.
14. Fay Vincent sent a memo to teams in 1991 stating that the use of steroids was illegal. It was a moral statement. Who knows how and if that memo was passed on to players and coaches. Barry Bonds could not have even gotten word of the memo for the first five years of his career, and substances were not officially banned until he was 40.

15. Yes, Pete Rose is officially banned for gambling. But it is naive to think that Pete didn't take every advantage he possibly could on the field, especially if he knew everyone around him was doing it.

16. Mays is Barry Bonds' godfather.

17. Many MLB players in the Hall of Fame have admitted to PED use, including Mays, Aaron, and Mantle.

18. Buck Showalter walked Barry Bonds with the bases loaded on May 28, 1998 when the Giants were playing the Arizona Diamondbacks. Arizona had a two run lead, and Showalter guessed it was better to give up one run than four.

19. An Oriole player who dropped dead in 2003 from organ failure brought on by PED use and the pressure to perform.

20. Baseball sent a memo. They did not change the rules or institute testing until 2005. That is clearly not standing up to conviction. They could easily have laid down the law.

21. He is probably better when comparing stats to many pitchers already in the Hall, like Jim Palmer, Bob Feller, Sandy Koufax, Dizzy Dean, Catfish Hunter, Bob Lemon, and Mike Mussina.

22. In an interview with *Sports Illustrated*, Tommy John spoke out against parents using him to help promote their children's careers in baseball.
    https://www.si.com/mlb/video/2019/03/05/tommy-john-speaks-out-against-tommy-john-surgery-youth-sports

23. Sang Ho Baek died in 2021 at the age of 20 following Tommy John. Any surgery comes with risk.

24. HGH shows benefits in recuperating from injury, but now that it is banned that benefit cannot be realized by any player. Just like PED use in young players was a reason to display a responsibility to the public.

25. Regardless of what you think about abortion and lobotomy, these procedures are restricted or banned in various countries and jurisdictions.

9

LARGER THAN LIFE AND GROWING IN MYTH

There are a lot of baseball stories that are hard to believe. Some players have more of the mystique of crazy than is likely their fair share. In this category, one player seems to stand practically alone on the stage when it comes to trying to separate truth from fiction. The storm of stories and antics that follow in his wake like debris from a tornado all together make him seem less real than even Sidd Finch.[1] It is this way because the reality of this player was already so large that it became possible to believe he would be capable of absolutely anything on or off the field.

Take the intellect of a 10-year-old, place it in the body of a hulking farm boy who has ADHD. Now give him an alcohol addiction and a lifelong love of fire engines that he was supposedly drawn to chase like a dog chasing cars. Let it sink in that he was a selfless, gentle, valiant man who saved the lives of thirteen or more people and one "drowning" log while unthinkingly putting his own life in danger as if he were indestructible. When a levee broke in Hickman, Kentucky that held back the mighty Mississippi, he jumped in like a superhero to help sandbag the gap as if he alone could stop the flow. When the gap was patched, he rowed for hours through the floodwaters looking for people in distress that he might save.[2] When the levee broke again the following year, he sacrificed himself again to move the river back to where it belonged—probably by just lifting it and putting it back in place. Never mind that the hours in the cold water and exhaustion from exertion gave him pneumonia that weakened his immunity which allowed him to contract tuberculosis that eventually claimed his life.

As kind and helpful as he was, he had at least one incident while carrying a gun that discharged accidentally. He beat his father-in-law badly with an iron because the man asked Rube for board that was owed. When the man's wife tried to stop Rube, he beat her away with a chair. Rube joined the circus to wrestle alligators in the offseason to fill his time,[3] and was the leading man in a vaudeville show. As he couldn't remember his lines he ad-libbed them every night to the delight of the audience and chagrin of the crew. While traveling with the show, he came to a town where there was a lion exhibition. When he went out of curiosity, he confronted the lion which either bit or swiped at him.[4] As he became known for crowd-pleasing, he later attempted a bigger stunt at an aquatic attraction by climbing in the tank with a walrus which he tried to hypnotize. He failed in the attempt and lost his trousers in the scuffle but emerged unharmed.[5]

"You can charm a manager, but you can't hypnotize a walrus."

— GEORGE "RUBE" WADDELL

His contract included a clause where he was forbidden to eat crackers in bed because his munching left his bed-mate losing sleep because of the crumbs. Connie Mack, the wise owner of the team Rube played for over much of his career, wouldn't pay him more than a few dollars at a time as it was the only way to control how much he drank. Rube was a fountain of unpredictability who was born on Friday the 13th and died on April Fool's day thirty-seven years later. Those dates, at least are no ruse.

Many of these anecdotes need to be considered a bit like taffy in that they have stretched and changed with time. Some parts of them may have been fabricated by a man who would be quickly dismissed from the stand by the worst of lawyers as being an unreliable witness to his own life. Just as he couldn't remember his lines as the lead of a play, he couldn't remember he'd not divorced his first wife before marrying his second. He sometimes forgot where he needed to be at game time, which didn't mean just the start time of the game, it may have meant which team he was supposed to play on and in which city. Freely following his muse to concentrate on what he was already involved in, he might be found fishing, playing games with kids, posing as a department store mannequin, or following a fire truck. These demonstrations of forgetfulness all put aside his copious craving for the mugs of beer and shots of delight that compromised the little brain power he naturally possessed.[6]

"He often missed school, but I could always find him playing ball, fishing, or following a fire engine."[7]

— RUBE WADDELL'S SISTER,
MARGARET

The swirl of misinformation surrounding Waddell continues to circulate, swell, and grow, which makes it hard to sift fact from fiction. Even when his adventures and accomplishments can be verified by newspapers, relatively reliable eye-witnesses, and box scores, they are sometimes amended with poetic license.

Some things are irrefutable in the record books. This same man spent ten solid seasons in the major leagues striking out 2,251 batters over 2,835 innings while winning 183 games.[8] Rube won the pitching triple crown in 1905[9] while missing an entire month of the season that would likely have extended his leading totals. In the end, his relatively short career was deemed good enough to gain election to the Hall of Fame.

"Good enough" is a bit of an understatement if you look at some of the particularly shining moments which solidified his image as a hero of the sport. He twice pitched both ends of a double-header (August 19, 1900 and August 21, 1903), accounting for a total of twenty-seven and seventeen innings in those appearances. Across those four starts, he went 3 and 1. In the 1900 twinbill, he pitched seventeen innings in the first game and was conned by his manager into pitching the second game with the reward of a fishing trip following the second game. Luckily the second game went only five innings before Rube was off on his trip.

These were iron-man accomplishments, but Waddell most admired and reveled in his outing against Cy Young on July 4, 1905. The game went twenty innings and both pitchers pitched a complete game with Waddell winning the game. After letting two runs be scored in the first, Waddell put up nineteen straight innings of goose eggs. It is rumored that a softly hit ball by Waddell drove in what was to be the winning run when it was misplayed in the top of the twentieth. The Boston Americans did make six errors on the day so the story is plausible even with Waddell showing no RBI on the day's box score. Boston did muster a threat in the bottom of the inning, but Waddell escaped the threat without letting up a run.

His nickname was "Rube," which refers to a farm boy who is stupid and lacks culture and manners. Hardly a compliment, the label was placed on him by a catcher during his short tour of the minor leagues. Most likely it was for his childlike manner, the fact that he was easily distracted, and his lack of knowledge about the game which he was not shy of displaying brilliantly. He never learned the basic rules, even though he'd played college ball on a scholarship. He went for the pay—rather than the academics—which was $2 a game, plus room and board.

"**Rube had a bad habit of throwing to bases without looking at the base to which he was throwing... the ball would go half a mile before it would be recovered, and every man who happened to be on the bases would score... he delighted in throwing to the basemen with all his strength.**"

— DR. THOMAS H. GEORGE,
MANAGER, VOLANT COLLEGE

Rube believed he could record an out by throwing the ball directly at a runner and hitting him rather than to the base where the runner was advancing. In one game, Waddell was batting in the eighth inning with a man on second. After a pitch, the catcher threw to second in a pick-off attempt and the ball sailed into the outfield. The A's runner took off and rounded third to score, and the center fielder fired home. Waddell, with bat still in hand, swung at the incoming throw and hit the ball back into play. He was called out for interference.

"They'd been feeding me curves all afternoon, and this was the first straight ball I'd looked at!"[10]

— RUBE WADDELL

One thing quite notable about Waddell was his outstanding arm. The is partially attributed to his brute strength from mining.[11] His accuracy may have something to do with his pastime of throwing stones at birds that gathered on the planted fields. It is understandable how throwing stones all day could have contributed to building his mighty endurance.

The love of fire trucks started at an early age and lasted through his life. It seems from various descriptions that he just felt the thrill and responsibility to be on hand in case he could jump in and save someone's life. Rumor suggests that he was witnessed running off the field during at least one game to chase a fire truck down the road to follow it to its destination. A lot of how he is portrayed as a person seems bent on making him a caricature and even more soft in the head than he may have actually been.

"Rube Waddell was the greatest pitcher in the game, and although widely known for his eccentricities, was more sinned against than sinner."

— CONNIE MACK

The problem with Rube's ever-growing legacy is that the stories began being fabricated even while he was still playing. Stories contained some elements of reality but writers either tended to embellish them or simply create fantasy. In the end, the lovable character's actual life ends up a soup of what is real, what is stretched, what is misread, and what is totally imaginary.

If you scour the internet, Waddell's history is practically treated like a set of Legos where he is assembled more by what will make him look funny and get likes than to take his legacy seriously. Every lie printed becomes a fact. One instance with an accidental discharge of his pistol in the lobby of a hotel becomes a story about how Rube plotted an attempt to murder his manager and good friend, Connie Mack. Facts are cherry-picked, unchecked, and end up printed for all to see just to perpetuate the mistakes and create new ones.[12] If he were scrapping with his father-in-law and the family dog jumped into the fray to defend his owner, Rube may have punched the dog to get him off after the dog bit Rube's pitching hand. That might be crossed up and morphed with Rube's visit to a lion on exhibition where Rube jumped into the cage and punched a lion instead. If one time he led a parade when he was supposed to be at the ballpark, in the minds of writers, he did it many times. And those are the stories that get fed to the voracious minds of the fans that swarm to the myth.

The trend to bend Rube's reality started at the very core of his history. For example, there was an article in Philadelphia's *North American*, from August 12, 1903, that reported this headline: "Rube Caused a Bean Factory to Blow Up." The event was fitted within the actual events of a baseball game on August 11 where Rube pitched and lost against the home team 5 to 1. Rube came to the plate according to the box score and batted three times. One of those may have been in the seventh inning. The story goes on to say how Waddell fouled off a ball in that inning of that game and the ball flew out of the stadium. It landed in Boston's largest bean cannery.[13] This is where reality left the stadium.

Apparently, the ball jammed in the steam whistle causing it to sound, which to most workers would have signaled quitting time. Hearing it go off, they began shutting down and heading toward the door. When the whistle didn't stop, neighboring factories began blasting their horns thinking it was some type of emergency. Panic ensued and workers rushed from the buildings without properly closing down their stations as the fire trucks, which had been summoned by police, began to arrive. One of the vats of beans—which the in the worker's haste to leave the building was left cooking and untended—over-heated and exploded. The explosion showered fans still in the stands nearest the factory with a scalding rain of beans and molasses. A fan, fearing for his life, deafened by the explosion, and torched by the searing rain went insane with panic during the deluge from the sky and shouted:

"The end of the world is coming and we will all be destroyed."

— ANONYMOUS BOSTON
AMERICANS' FAN

There were some strange footnotes about this story starting with the fact that the Philadelphia paper was the only newspaper in the country to carry the story. There is no record of a bean factory explosion reported on that date in Boston in any popular news source or record. Rube was not reported to have run out of the stadium chasing the sound of the sirens and the fire trucks to the place he would be needed to save humanity as he would have been in the commotion even if he were pitching the game. Oh, and the story was penned by Charles Dryden. Dryden was considered a masterful sports humorist during his time writing for the paper. Even in the accounting above, I have had a hand in smoothing out the rough edges of the events described in the article just to maintain the tradition.[14]

Regardless of the fact that it can be proven to be false with relative ease, the bean incident is reported now in accounts of Waddell's legacy as the truth when "researchers" find it and fail to look below the surface. Rest assured that many more of the "facts" you can dig up about Waddell are false and morphed and probably not as endearing or important as the reality of the man who earned the respect of his fellow players by being great at the game. In the end, even a heartfelt message that was supposedly crafted for young baseball fans is in question.

> "I had my chance, and a good one it was. Many boys may have a better one ahead of them than I had. If they will leave the booze alone, they won't have any trouble. I am not a very good preacher, but... keep away from booze and cigarettes."[15]
>
> — RUBE WADDELL

This message sounds virtually the same as one given by Hack Wilson on the radio just days before his death, and similar to one by Mickey Mantle expressing his regrets of excess. There also seems to be no record of who the recipient of this letter was. Regretfully, the origin is in as much doubt as much of the rest of his story and his last words to teammates as he lay dying.

> "I'll be over tomorrow and show you bums how to run. My weight is down to fighting trim now. I'm in shape."
>
> — RUBE WADDELL

In the end, what holds is his place in the Hall of Fame, and the numbers in the box scores. Those markers are no myth.

----

1. Something needs to be said here about the general recklessness of research that exists on the internet for this particular character. The fluid imagination—even by authors who are supposed to represent his life faithfully in biographies—seems to be willing to make this particular player into a bigger circus than he already is.
2. *The Hickman Courier*, Thursday, April 4, 1912.
3. Macht, Norman L., 2007. *Connie Mack and the Early Years of Baseball.*
4. October 31, 1903 *Cincinnati Enquirer*. This account is considered questionable as it conflicts with other reporting and Waddell's own recounting.
5. *The Wilkes-Barre Record*, Thursday, March 28, 1912.
6. At least one resource notes that Waddell did well in school: https://pabook.libraries.psu.edu/literary-cultural-heritage-map-pa/bios/Waddell__Rube
7. There is remarkably little information about Waddell's family.
8. This is inclusive of only 1900 to 1909. Over that period Cy Young struck out 1,365, pitched 3,341 innings, and won 231 games.
9. 27 Wins, 1.48 ERA, 287 Ks.
10. Unconfirmed response.
11. Some accounts say Waddell lived and worked on a family farm, but his father was in the oil industry. The town he lived in was a farming community. This is the kind of fact that readily gets jumbled.
12. William Braund calls his book about Waddell, *King of the Hall of Flakes*, a novel. The reason for that is because it is mostly fiction. He takes complete liberty with the facts or doesn't even bother with them. Many people will pick up his work thinking it is a biography and reference. It isn't.
13. Boston's baked beans were a thing, which is why a Boston team was named the Beaneaters.

14. A resource online does have a clipping of the original article as well as a breakdown of some investigation into its validity. Find that here:

    https://www.thefreelibrary.com/Consider+your+sources%
    3A+baseball+and+baked+beans+in+Boston.-a0144201875

15. Alan Levy, *Rube Waddell: The Zany, Brilliant Life of a Strikeout Artist*

10

I NEVER SAID MOST OF THE THINGS I SAID

I magine being one of the best players ever to play your position in the history of baseball and having your career take a back seat to some words you supposedly said. It is almost a tragedy. This baseball oddity quit school at a young age to go to work and help support his family by working in a shoe factory. He later said he'd still be there if it wasn't for baseball. He enlisted to serve in the Navy and earned a Purple Heart in WWII after being wounded on the beaches at Normandy and missed two years of his career due to service.

In his seventeen-year career, this star played in fourteen World Series, helping to win ten titles—the most by any player in baseball history. Playing in a record 75 World Series games, he contributed with more than just the twelve home runs he hit in those fall classics. He was a fifteen-time All-Star[1] and three-time AL MVP. He shares the distinction of winning three MVP awards with such well-known stars as Mickey Mantle, Joe DiMaggio, Stan Musial, Jimmie Foxx, Mike Schmidt, Alex Rodriguez, Albert Pujols, Roy Campanella, and Mike Trout.[2] His player stats for the regular season include a lifetime .285 batting average, 358 home runs, 2,150 hits, and 1,430 RBIs. He was inducted into the Hall of Fame in 1972.

Barely remembered for his exclusive talent on the field, this guy struck out only 414 times over 7,555 at-bats. He was considered an amazing "bad-ball" hitter and somehow combined a relatively tiny five-foot-seven frame with power and contact to become an offensive force.

"[People said to me] you're a bad-ball hitter. No, the ball looked good to me [so I hit it]."

— LAWRENCE "YOGI" BERRA

Through the course of his career, he moved from player to player-manager and finally ended up managing the Yankees in 1964 bringing them all the way to the World

Series. That year they lost to St. Louis but it took all seven games. Then in 1973, Yogi managed the team across town: the New York Mets. They sat in last place in the division until August 30. Questioned by a reporter in July if the season was over, Yogi made a sort of prophecy.

"It ain't over till it's over."

— LAWRENCE "YOGI" BERRA

The Mets went from last place to first and clinched the division on their second to last game of the season, taking the division in front of the surging Cardinals who won their final five games. Moving on to the World Series, Berra's "Ya Gotta Believe"[3] Mets went the full seven games in the series outscoring the A's, but losing in the final game 5 to 2. These successes just added to the record number of times he reached the World Series.

What is the player who has appeared in the most World Series as a player and manager remembered for?

"I wish I had an answer to that because I'm tired of answering that question."

— LAWRENCE "YOGI" BERRA

Accidental philosophic and paradoxical quips, his welcoming demeanor and a TV commercial promotion with a duck.

The Four Balls Story (An introduction to Yogi-isms as told by Whitey Ford)[4]

"The White Sox came into Yankee Stadium in '59 and I was pitching ... Up comes Luis Aparicio. The first pitch I throw to him he bunts down third, beats it out. One pitch, man on first. Nellie Fox gets up; first pitch, double down the left-field line. Two pitches, second and third. Minnie Minoso, I threw him a really good curveball but it hit him in the kneecap, so he walks down to first. I've thrown three pitches and the bases are loaded. And up comes Ted Kluszewski... First pitch, high fastball off the right-center field wall. Three runs scored. I have thrown four pitches. Casey comes out to the mound and Yogi doesn't want to miss that, so he gets out there. Casey says to Yogi: "Does Ford have anything tonight?" and Yogi says: "How the hell do I know, I haven't caught a pitch yet!"

"Ninety percent of the game [of baseball] is half mental."

— YOGI BERRA

On the field, behind the plate, Yogi flapped his gums. A lot. He talked to the players in the batter's box and with the umpires, casually stirring up a dialogue. Yogi was kind and personable, yet in his subtle manner, he used his conversations to the advantage of his team. He might ask a player about their family, wonder what they had for lunch. Then when Yogi had made them comfortable, he might say what he called "helpful things." He might warn them that the pitcher was a little wild that day and seem concerned with their personal safety. In a teasing way, he might try to convince them to step back from the plate a little or to be careful not to lose sight of the ball in the white of the pitcher's uniform as the ball sailed toward them.

He admitted to once trying to get thrown out of a game by riding the umpire. Why? Because it was hot and his team was winning by a lot and he didn't want to be there anymore.

"When you come to a fork in the road, take it."[5]

— YOGI BERRA

One of the most popular Yogi-isms was supposed to have been said one of the ten times in 1961 where Mickey Mantle and Roger Maris hit back-to-back home runs. During the 1961 season, Maris and Mantle were having a duel to chase what was then thought to be an insurmountable record of sixty home runs in a single season, smacked by Babe Ruth in 1927.[6] In Yogi's classic style, his reaction to one of the ten back-to-back performances would certainly be the type of malapropism that he would effortlessly coin. But like many things from the lore of baseball, there is rumor and no record to substantiate it.

"It's deja vu all over again."[7]

— YOGI BERRA

Once Yogi had become known for his quips, he continued to distort language into humorous kaleidoscopes. Having gained a reputation for his use of language, people were always on the lookout for him to say something clever and thought he could just make up Yogi-isms on the spot. Probably because people kept an ear out for his whimsy, the library of his quotes grew and he ended up getting credit for a lot of things he never said.[8] True to his form and under the constant scrutiny, his persona would come out with a language-twisting phrase when no one was expecting it. It brought him a lot of attention in the press and won him contracts for product endorsements.

"Can you cut the pizza in four pieces? I'm not hungry enough to eat six."[9]

— YOGI BERRA

One such endorsement left Yogi a bit miffed. He was signed to do a commercial with an insurance company called Aflac that used a duck as a brand mascot. The talking duck was somewhat mischievous and said the name of the company instead of quacking. The company wanted to use Yogi-isms in their scripting to inject some additional humor into the plot of their commercials.

By this time (2002), Yogi was getting up in age but still enjoyed working with the guys in spring training and continuing his life-long journey with his love for the game. He was not at all pleased to find out he had to take a break from the team to fly out to California for a Friday shoot and he let it show.

On the morning Yogi found out about the commercial, Ron Guidry went to pick him up to take Yogi to spring training as he usually did. Guidry acted as Yogi's chauffeur[10] during spring training for years, and he could tell Yogi was upset. He usually waved to everyone and smiled as he walked out of the hotel but was clearly in a grumpy mood and cursing as he got into the car. Guidry asked Yogi what was wrong and Yogi said:

"I got to fly to LA... to make an affliction commercial."

— YOGI BERRA

Guidry was a bit puzzled wondering what affliction Yogi was talking about and began to drive off toward the stadium. As Guidry was trying to figure out what question to ask, Yogi turned to him and said:

"You know, with that goddamn duck!"

— YOGI BERRA

Guidry began laughing so hard that he practically lost control of the truck. He pulled off and asked Yogi if he meant Aflac. He and Yogi had a good laugh before getting back on the road.

When Yogi came back from the trip, Guidry was there to pick him up at the airport. He asked Yogi how it went and Yogi looked at Guidry and said:

"Gator.[11] You realize that duck really doesn't talk?"

— YOGI BERRA

Everyone seemed to have their own stories about Yogi as if his wellspring of accidental insight were inspirational. George Bush, famed for his clumsy presidential speeches, claimed people thought Yogi was one of his scriptwriters. Reggie Jackson remembers standing next to Yogi at an old-timers' game as they scrolled through the names of baseball greats who had died that year as a final farewell. Yogi tugged at Reggie to get his attention and said:

"I hope I never see my name up there."

— YOGI BERRA

Yogi's legacy ends up not being just his accomplishments on the field. It ends up being his dedication to his country, team, family, and friends. It is about sitting by the bedside of Phil Rizzuto as he lay in an assisted living facility; watching over him in his final days and sharing stories that may not have been perfectly remembered. He spent the last moments of his life-long teammate's final hours playing cards and comforting him playing the game of life the only way he knew how.

Yogi is a celebration of living life to the fullest, enjoying the moment, and spreading his kindness, humility, and innocence. He was one small man who became bigger than baseball and a champion of life, living, and respect.

"You should always go to other people's funerals, otherwise they won't come to yours."

— YOGI BERRA

1. He actually played in eighteen all-star games as there were two in 1959, 1960, and 1961.
2. Trout still has plenty of time to tack on another award.
3. The Mets had a surprise run to the World Series in 1969 with the slogan "The Miracle Mets," and again the Mets fans latched on to the underdog.
4. This account (https://youtu.be/aiJSpq6v-GY) is apparently of a game on April 30, which is the only one that comes close to what happened. Whitey gets just about every possible detail wrong beside the fact that Luis Aparicio bunted a single to third and that he hit a player on the third pitch (Jim Landis). First of all, they were in Chicago, not New York. Aparicio got on with the bunt, and then Nellie Fox grounded out to second base and Aparicio advanced on a fielder's choice. Whitey hit only one player that year, and it was in this game, but it was not Minnie Minoso. Although Minoso led the league in getting hit ten times in his thirteen full seasons in MLB, he was playing for Cleveland in '58 and '59 between two stints with the White Sox. The fourth pitch went to Ray Boone, not Ted Kluszewski. Boone had only 21 at-bats for the White Sox that year. Kluszewski did play for the Sox in '59, but was only on the team after August 25. The one game Kluszewski faced Whitey Ford was on September 15. He got a walk and a single in four plate appearances. No doubles. Ford also faced the Sox at Yankee stadium on May 15 and Aparicio and Fox were on third and second in the first inning, but Landis grounded out. Aparicio scored on a fielder's choice. Yogi's version of the same story is different (https://youtu.be/rCqrvLBQxwo?t=932). Yogi

claimed that Fox hit a single when the bases were loaded because the next guy got hit and the fourth hit a grand slam. So Yogi said four runs scored in that same story.

5. Directions he gave to his boyhood friend, Joe Garagiola, to get to his house. While Joe was a friend and player, he became more well-known for his own crusades as a baseball announcer and baseball blooper reels. He was instrumental in perpetuating the promotion of Yogi's quips.

6. People like to debate whether the record was really challenged, because in 1961 the season was lengthened to 162 games from 154. Maris hit #61 on the final day of the 162 game season.

7. Supposedly Berra referring to the fact that Maris and Mantle frequently went back-to-back that season.

8. The title of this chapter refers to a quote that Yogi used more than once to express the idea that people ultimately put words in his mouth.

9. Yogi was ordering a pizza and the waitress asked how he wanted it cut.

10. The adventures were chronicled in a book called *Driving Mr. Yogi*.

11. Ron Guidry's nickname.

JARABE TAPATÍO, OR DANCING AROUND THE GOLDEN SOMBRERO

This chapter is here for stat nerds. It is the sole *raison d'etre*. If you hate statistics, skip to the next chapter.

Striking out four times in a game is such a notorious flop that baseball has a sarcastic and spirited name for the achievement. It is called the Golden Sombrero.[1] A sombrero is often associated with its negative stereotype of a lazy Mexican having a siesta with his wide-brimmed hat pulled down over his face to shade him from the sun as he sleeps in the afternoon. Maybe that stereotype of "asleep at the plate" was what Carmelo Martinez was thinking when he was credited with coining the term.[2] According to lore, he had a particularly bad day at the plate and is said to have kept his sense of humor when interviewed by a reporter.

"[That was a] big hat trick... a sombrero... probably made of gold."[3]

— CARMELO MARTINEZ

Somehow his words were remembered and spread through locker rooms and polished with time. The achievement of a Golden Sombrero lends levity to a ballplayer's failure. It reflects a bad day at the plate and has achieved a name and recognition. A more notorious and rare "achievement" is not distinguished with a name, and that is hitting into four double plays in a single game. That means that in just four swings a single player accounts for 30 percent of a team's outs for the day.

The difference is that you have to swing and hit into a double play. In a samurai way, it is more honorable to hit into an out, even if it is more than one of them. A player can strike out by hitting the snooze button. Striking out does less to kill a rally. Achieved only three times, hitting into four double plays might be called offensive indifference.

- Goose Goslin, April 28, 1934, killed four Detroit rallies and ended each inning taking his turn at bat to whack groundballs to the right of the diamond and contribute more than his share of the outs. Despite Goslin's best efforts to thwart his team's chances of winning, Detroit won the game 4 to 1 over Cleveland.

- Joe Torre, July 21, 1975, completely killed only two rallies by ending the inning with his batted balls. The Mets failed to score in each of the innings where Torre contributed two-thirds of the outs while effectively negating Felix Millan's otherwise very productive 4-for-4 day at the plate (Millan was always the runner who was forced out). The Mets were probably not surprised to lose to the Astros 6 to 2.

- On September 11, 2011, Víctor Martínez killed two potential rallies by ending the inning but with slightly more style than the other two players in this exclusive club. He at least managed a line-out into an unassisted double play along with his three ground ball inning killers. One of his groundouts scored a run, though he was not credited with an RBI because of an error on the previous play.

Two of these players are already in the Hall of Fame, so you don't necessarily have to be a chump to ground into a double play.

Achieving the shameful badge of the Golden Sombrero has become more frequent in the era of the home run when it seems each at-bat is an all-or-nothing escapade of putting the ball over the fence or striking out—as if nothing else mattered. Hits outnumbered strikeouts in every season until 2017 where there were 2,111 more hits than strikeouts. Then the strikeouts outpaced hits for the next four years.

Year	Hits	Strikeouts	Strikeouts Exceeded Hits By
2018	41,018	41,207	189
2019	42,039	42,823	784
2020	14,439	15,586	1,147
2021	39,481	42,145	2,664

Strikeouts are becoming so popular that new names have been invented to describe the spectacular achievements of being unable to put the ball in play. Striking out five times in a game is called a Platinum Sombrero. Striking out six times in a game is a Titanium Sombrero.[4]

Aaron Judge once struck out eight times on June 4, 2018, using both ends of a double-header to perform that feat. Eight strikeouts in one day seems to deserve a name of its own. In one of those two games he earned a Platinum Sombrero which is another rare feat of striking out five times in a nine-inning game. No one has ever struck out more in one day than Judge did during that double-header.

It comes as no surprise that the players who have so far achieved the most Golden Sombreros is a list of power-hitting one-trick ponies. If they hit it, it goes a long way. If not, they whiff. Ryan Howard has the most Golden Sombreros as of this writing with 27. Chris Davis Follows close behind with 26. Their lifetime stat lines are remarkably similar.

Another strikeout award that is not named is one that was achieved by Joe Sewell. In 1925, 1929, 1930, 1932, and 1933, Sewell struck out five times (or less).[5] Five times or less—over the course of an entire season. It was not some statistical anomaly where he played a limited number of games. During these five seasons he averaged 513 at-bats. In other words, it took him all of 1932 and 1933[6] to strike out one less time than Aaron Judge did in one day in 2018. Sewell repeated that same spread of striking out only seven times in 1929 and 1930.

"It was just a simple matter of keeping my eye on the ball."

— JOE SEWELL

In 7,132 official at-bats (8,333 plate appearances) during his career, Sewell struck out a total of 114 times. The average strikeout rate for all of MLB in 2021 was one strikeout per 3.84 at-bats. Over the course of 513 at-bats in one year, the average 2021 player would strike out 133 times, or nineteen more times than Sewell did in his entire fourteen-year career.

- Trea Turner led all of MLB with a .328 AVE and 195 hits in 2021. He struck out 110 times in 595 at-bats. He was awarded a Golden Sombrero for his performance on May 31.
- Juan Soto led all of MLB with a rather ridiculous .465 on-base percentage. He struck out only ninety-three times in 502 official at-bats. He never won a sombrero but did have three hat tricks (three strikeouts in one game) on three occasions.
- Kevin Newman—hardly a star—led the majors in at-bats per strikeout in 2021. He kept his grand whiff total to only 42 Ks in 517 at-bats which amounts to 1 strikeout every 12.6 at-bats. His rate is two at-bats better than the nearest contender (David Fletcher, 60 Ks in 626 at-bats). Still, there were five times Newman struck out twice in a game. Sewell struck out

twice in a game a total of two times in his career. It happened seven years apart.

The list of great players who never achieved a Golden Sombrero is relatively long and includes some of the greatest players of all time along with some of the most recognized power hitters: Babe Ruth, Hank Aaron, Lou Gehrig, Ted Williams, Ty Cobb, Honus Wagner, Joe DiMaggio—and even current stars like Albert Pujols. None come close to Sewell's ability to put the ball in play. The closest runner-up in the history of post-1900 baseball[7] was Lloyd Waner who struck out 173 times in 7,772 at-bats, or 50 percent more than Sewell.

"[In 1925], I had a record. I went to bat 600 times. I struck out four times. I didn't swing at three of the four. One was a bad call. [The pitcher] threw a ball right at my cap bill and [the umpire] Bill McGowan said: 'Strike three you're out—oh my god, I missed it!' He came up and apologized to me the next day."[8]

— JOE SEWELL

Sewell claimed he could see so well that he saw the spiraling seams on a baseball when pitched and watched the ball come off his bat. The one bat he used for his entire career was a 40-ounce bat modeled after one used by Shoeless Joe Jackson throughout his career. These bats were made of wood from the north side of a hickory tree and stained with tobacco juice. Sewell's one Black Betsy lasted through all fourteen years of his career.

As the art of contact hitting fades into history as a lost art in the game, it looks like there's no need to name the achievement of striking out only four times over 600 at-bats as it probably will never happen again. The award might as well be known as "a Joe Sewell."

---

1. The Mexican hat dance is typically a symbol of pride and romance.
2. Some reports say he struck out four times, but that isn't correct. He had two games in 1984 where he struck out three times. In both those games he had at least one hit and one RBI. 1988 was the only time he struck out four times as a pro and that was long after the term had been used in print.
3. The Cub's Leon Durham was quoted by Steve Daley using the term saying that he was happy to have escaped winning a golden sombrero by hitting a triple and walking in his fourth and fifth at-bats after striking out in his first three plate appearances in a game on April 13, 1984.
4. Also known as a Double-Platinum Sombrero and a Horn, named after Sam Horn of the Baltimore Orioles achieved this in an extra inning game (fifteen) on July 17, 1991. It took him eight plate appearances that included a walk, reaching base on a strikeout(!),

and hitting a double. Eight players have achieved the feat of striking out six times in a game. All of those were extra innings.

5. Statistical comparison between game logs and Sewell's totals show an inconsistency. Sewell has five strikeouts in the game logs, but is credited with only four in his totals according to baseball-reference.com.

6. During these years Sewell was with the Yankees and roomed with Lou Gehrig.

7. Wee Willie Keeler, playing from 1892 to 1910 did manage only 136 times in 8,591 at-bats. He had one year where he edged out Sewell in striking out only two times in 570 at-bats in 1899. However he also had the advantage of different rules that helped him achieve his record.

8. From an Oral History recording of Joe Sewell, August 1, 1986. https://collection.baseballhall.org/islandora/object/ islandora%3A268693

12

105 GAMES WITHOUT TOUCHING
A BAT, A GLOVE, OR A BALL

There comes a time when a chapter has to be as short as a player's career, or at least fitting to the depth of skills he had in playing the game.

Of course, there were infamous players whose baseball careers were really short. The one at-bat career of Eddie Gaedel was probably the shortest if taken by all standards. Standing at three feet, seven inches, Gaedel was paid—minimum wage, of course—to take the field on August 19, 1951, for the St. Louis Browns. Sporting the number 1/8, the smallest positive number ever on a jersey in baseball history,[1] Gaedel was given a specific role to play. The manager, Zack Taylor, instilled confidence in our hero—as he tied the man's shoes like a father holding a small boy in his lap—that he need not fear that the other team would throw at him.[2] General

Manager Bill Veeck went a step further in cementing what Gaedel was paid to do. He warned Gaedel to crouch as they'd practiced, and not attempt heroics at the plate by moving the bat off his shoulder.

"I was an expert rifleman in the Marines, and I have a rifle up [on the roof]. When you get in that ball game today, if you swing that bat, I'll shoot you dead."[3]

— BILL VEECK

Veeck's words promised that Gaedel's career would be even shorter had he gone even slightly off-script.

Fearing for his life, Gaedel was sent in to pinch-hit for the first batter in the bottom of the first inning in the second game of the double-header. Gaedel took his curtain call, and the defense took a huddle wondering how to play a little person. The catcher lay on the ground to get his target low enough, and the grumpy umpire would have nothing to do with making a mockery of the game. No, this was pushing the limits far enough.

Detroit's Bob Cain threw four pitches that sailed past Gaedel's eyes that would have been strikes for any normal-sized player. Gaedel just sat and watched the balls fly by until he was told to take his base by the ump. He stopped several times on the way to bow to the admiring crowd which had roared into a frenzy. When he arrived at first, he was promptly lifted from the game for a pinch-runner. It could have only been slightly funnier if he played for the Giants.

But in this short chapter, we are not talking about Eddie, who at least touched a bat and took a plate appearance in his major league debut. We can put aside the sequel to his first appearance where he was put on a baseball field to play an alien in a staged abduction of players on the White Sox.[4] What we are talking about instead is a man who played a total of 105 major league games, scored 33 runs, stole 31 bases, and was a member of the 1974 World Champion Oakland Athletics. He never touched a bat, a glove, or a ball. He never stood at the plate, never threw a pitch, and never played in the field. All he really did was act as substitute legs for other players. With those opportunities, he achieved a few average base-running stats while creating some unnecessary outs. And for that, he earned a World Series ring.

"He's the only man in baseball—and it could only happen with the Oakland ball club—where they hire a man to do nothing but run."

— CURT GOWDY

Herb Washington was signed by the Oakland A's who took him on strictly for his speed. He was a sprinter who broke the world record for the 50- and 60-yard dashes several times in his track and field career.

Ready to sign his contract to play speedster for the A's, his contract negotiation was held back by a small detail. He was going to be signed to a $45,000 deal with a $20,000 signing bonus with one caveat.

"You have to grow a mustache by opening day and I'll give you another $2,000."[5]

— CHARLIE FINLEY

Washington was unable to grow much facial hair and his mustache, by opening day of spring training, was little more than a feathering. His sister offered the advice that he just "pencil it in" with makeup as women did with their eyebrows. Herb gave it a try, but when the bench manager inspected him for the bonus, he told Herb that the mustache was not credible.

Later that day Herb extorted some resources and went back to visit the bench coach again. He waived $200 at him, then asked him to take another look at the mustache which he must not have seen in good light. The manager somehow now saw the mustache as passable—prominent even—and Herb ended up winning his bonus money for the small bribe.

Regretfully, what Herb was able to conjure up as a clever manipulator of circumstance, he was not able to deal on the base paths. His speed did win him 31 stolen bases but over a total of 48 attempts. That's 17 outs for anyone counting. In the end, he was 1/10 of 1 percent better at stealing than the league average. His performance in the postseason led to a total of five appearances recording two caught stealing attempts, one pickoff, and no other offensive production except being the out in a fielder's choice.

In other words, his only benefit to the A's winning effort in the World Series was to record three or more outs. One in pinch-running for Reggie Jackson and making the first out in the eighth inning of a three-run inning in a 5 to 0 win over the Orioles. The second was pinch-running for Gene Tenace who stole a base in the previous game during the inning where Herb was thrown out.[6] The third was picked off for unsound base running skills.

The crowning achievement of Herb's visit to the post-season was in Game 2 of the World Series against the Dodgers. Behind 3 to 0, the A's scored two runs in the ninth inning when Sal Bando got hit by a pitch and Reggie Jackson doubled. Joe Rudi hit a single to score Bando and Jackson. Rudi, on first, represented the tying run. After Gene Tenace struck out for the first out of the inning, Rudi, not known for his speed, got lifted for Herb who pinch-ran for him. Herb got picked off first base, effectively ending the rally by making the second out and clearing the bases. Angel Mangual, pinch-hitting for Blue Moon Odom, struck out ending the game with the Dodgers winning by a run.

Oakland won the next three games and took the series despite the fact that Herb appeared two more times. He pinch-ran for Gene Tenace in the third game to no benefit as the next two batters made unproductive outs. He also pinch-ran for Jim Holt and got forced out in a fielder's choice in the fourth game (effectively another base-running out, but let's not be picky).

Eddie Gaedel may have been a little person, a Martian, and a parody, but he had a 1.000 on-base percentage and never sapped a rally. Herb Washington was a failure as a baseball player but holds world records, had a successful career as a McDonald's franchise owner, sports the only Topps baseball card where the position is Pinch Runner, and is the only player in major league baseball who has appeared in more than one hundred games, yet never held a bat, never touched a ball, never played the field as a defender, and has a World Series ring.

---

1. Several players have worn the number zero or double zero.
2. Peter Golenbock, *The Spirit of St. Louis: A History of the St. Louis Cardinals and Browns*
   St. Louis sportswriter Bob Broeg
3. Veeck speaking to Gaedel.
4. Bill Veeck put four little people in alien costumes and had them abduct players from the White Sox team during the game.
5. This part of the story comes directly from a recorded interview available in various places around the internet and can be verified in Herb's own words. https://youtu.be/LVkigDj0HEw
6. In the same pitching and catching battery, Tenace stole a base. Tenace was 36 for 78 stealing bases in his entire fifteen-year career.

13

FIRED FOR A SONG

Sometimes a different kind of champion steps on the field. Billy Martin was not a great baseball player. He was cherished by some as a teammate because of his scrappy, clutch playing style when he was on the field. In 1953, he was the World Series' MVP putting up 12 hits in the six-game series, batting .500 with 8 RBI. He ended the series by knocking in the winning run with one out in the bottom of the ninth in the final game. That year he was a force in pushing the Yankees to win a record fifth straight World Series. At the age of 25, he was playing on a team with many future Hall of Fame players like Mickey Mantle, Yogi Berra, Whitey Ford, Phil Rizzuto, Johnny Mize, and Casey Stengel, and he lifted them on his shoulders and lived the dream of every child who swings a bat in a game of their imagination.

"I'd rather be a Yankee than the president of the United States."

— BILLY MARTIN

He played with the New York Yankees from 1950 to 1957 on teams that made appearances in five World Series, and they won four of those under the leadership of Casey Stengel. But almost as if his meteoric rise had caused him to use everything he had in the tank, his career started to sputter. Management saw his scrapping and drinking off the field was negatively influencing his teammates and especially his roommate Mantle. During a trip to Kansas City on June 15 during the 1957 campaign, Martin got traded to the Kansas City A's between the first and second games of the series and was set to switch dugouts the next day. He, Mickey Mantle, and Whitey Ford sat up all night drinking and reminiscing until dawn about the legendary run these friends, teammates, and brothers had in their years together in the game.

Martin played for four more years and five more teams, seeming to always get moved because of his rough-housing and because he rubbed management the wrong way. But leaving his Yankees behind took some of the spirit from his play. After his eleventh year, his career as a player ended in 1961 at the age of 33 when he was released by the Twins.

"I've got the reputation for being baseball's bad boy and I don't deserve it... I think I'd make a good manager... I know enough about the game... Unfortunately, I don't think I'll ever get the chance and there's nothing in the world that can change that."

— BILLY MARTIN, *BASEBALL DIGEST*, JUNE 1961

It turns out Billy was wrong. He went on to manage five different teams over sixteen years, getting fired eight times over that span. It takes a special kind of attitude to get fired eight times by five teams. It was almost nine, but in one instance he quit before it happened.

One moment that helps define Martin's personal lore and personality came in one of his many documented and fabled off-field exploits. Mickey Mantle wanted to bring Billy out to hunt with a new gun he'd been given. Mickey had a friend who owned some land so the two took a four-hour drive out to the ranch.[1] When they got there, Mickey went up to the doctor's door and asked his permission to go hunting. The doctor agreed but asked Mickey to do him a favor and put down an old mule that was aging and had gone blind. Mickey agreed and then decided to pull a prank on Martin who was still in the car.

When Mickey returned to the car he acted upset that they'd taken the trip for nothing. The doctor didn't want them hunting on his land. Mickey took his gun and told Martin he was going to kill the doctor's mule. Martin tried to convince Mantle that it was a really bad idea, but Mantle insisted and walked off toward the barn and put down the mule. A moment later Mantle heard a few shots and found Martin with his smoking gun. Martin, always the team player, told Mantle he killed two of the doctor's cows. Mantle was left to explain his prank and Billy was left to pay for the cows.[2]

"[Those cows] cost me $800."

— BILLY MARTIN

Billy's first tour as manager started with the Twins in 1969. In 1968, the Twins finished in seventh place, twenty-four games out of the running. Looking for a change and noting Martin's success as a manager of their minor league affiliate, Calvin Griffith offered the big-league job to Martin. Continuing his aggressive style, Martin led the Twins to first place in the first year of division play.

"I feel like I'm sitting on a keg of dynamite."

— CALVIN GRIFFITH, GIVING HIS
IMPRESSION OF MARTIN AS A
MANAGER

Even though the Twins took first place under Martin in 1969, management felt Martin's risk outweighed his benefit and did not sign him for 1970.

Martin spent 1970 out of baseball, and Jim Campbell signed Martin to take the helm of the ailing Detroit Tigers in 1971 which had a star-studded lineup that underperformed in the previous two years. Martin led the team to a second-place finish in 1971, first in 1972, and third in 1973. But Martin was already gone before the end of the '73 season. With twenty-eight games left to play, Martin encouraged his pitchers to throw spitballs in protest of umpires not calling Gaylord Perry for throwing the illegal pitch. Martin went on record with the press, was suspended by the AL president, and before the suspension was over, Martin was dismissed from his responsibilities as manager.

Bob Short, owner of the Texas Rangers saw Martin's release as a great opportunity. In a back-handed apology, Short told his current manager Whitey Herzog that he would fire his own grandmother to have a chance to hire Martin. Days later Herzog was dismissed when Martin was hired, inheriting a team that had stumbled to a 47 and 81 record. The team finished in last place.

"I'm fired. I'm the grandmother."

— WHITEY HERZOG

In 1974, Martin changed the prospects of the Rangers considerably. They finished second in the league with an 84 and 76 record, improving by twenty-seven wins. But the team was sold by Short to Jim Corbett at the beginning of the season. Corbett was much more hands-on than Short and reduced Martin's managerial control. Corbett also found Martin's behavior and attitude difficult to deal with. Their grievances with each other continued to mount and came to a head on July 20 of 1975, the day after Corbett told Martin he was considering firing him. Corbett obviously did not understand that Martin wasn't one to fool with.

"Billy is the only guy in the world who can hear someone give him the finger."

— **MICKEY MANTLE**

Martin stewed over the threat and an issue from earlier in the season bubbled up to the surface. In the sixth inning of the next game, Martin called the public address announcer and demanded that he play "Thank God I'm a Country Boy" instead of the traditional "Take Me Out to the Ball Game," during the seventh-inning stretch. This was something Martin and Corbett argued about at the beginning of the season, and Corbett insisted on the more traditional song rather than Martin's push for what would please the crowd. Corbett blew up when the song came on and fired Billy immediately after the game.

By this time, one positive aspect of Martin's reputation was his ability to turn a ball club around. Because of that reputation, Martin was hired by George Steinbrenner for his first tour as manager of the Yankees. Billy led the team to a pennant in 1976, and then to a World Series win in 1977, all the while battling with Steinbrenner and the new "star" Steinbrenner hired in the likes of Reggie Jackson. A summary of the events seems in order.

- Reggie claims to be "the straw that stirs the drink," suggesting disrespect for both Martin and team Captain Thurman Munson.
- On June 18, in a nationally televised game against the Red Sox, the Yankees trailed 4 to 7 having fallen half a game out of first place on the previous day's loss. Martin felt Jackson didn't hustle on a one-out base hit by Jim Rice, turning the single into a double. Instead of it being one-out with first and second, it was one out with second and third. During a pitching change, Martin lifted Jackson before another

pitch was thrown, replacing him with Paul Blair to show up Jackson, and a well-known altercation ensued.[3]

- Jackson hit three homers on three pitches from three different pitchers, winning the sixth and final game of the World Series to become a legend of the postseason. His stats that year earned him the nickname Mr. October.

- In the 1978 season, with the Yankees tied 5 to 5 in the tenth inning of a game against Kansas City, Martin gave the sign to have Jackson put down a sacrifice bunt after Munson hit a lead-off single. Jackson became defiant and bunted the next two pitches ignoring the signs to swing away, even after a visit from the third-base coach. He popped out to the catcher on the third pitch and may have cost the Yankees the game because his ego was bigger than the team.

- Martin called for Jackson's suspension for the rest of the season for ignoring signs but Jackson only got five games. Martin learned from Bill Veeck that Steinbrenner was trying to work a manager swap with the White Sox, and on the advice of his lawyer, quit on July 24, 1978, before he was traded or fired. This meant the Yankees had to pay him.

- Steinbrenner almost immediately regretted

pushing Billy, and after hiring Bob Lemon to a two-year contract, brought Billy back for Old-Timers' Day just five days after he resigned. The Yankees announced Martin as their new manager for 1980, leaving Lemon as a lame duck.

- Martin came back early after the Yankees got off to a sour start in 1979, and got fired later that year five days after having a brawl with a marshmallow salesman who he mocked because of his profession.

"All I know is, I pass people on the street [of New York City] these days, and they don't know whether to say hello or to say good-bye."

— BILLY MARTIN

- Hired by the Oakland A's before the 1980 season and true-to-form, he turned the team around going from dead last in '79 to a respectable second-place in '80. In 1981, the season was split by a strike, and the A's took first place in the first half, but later lost to the Yankees in a three-game sweep. 1982 did not go well, and rumor had it that he'd been contacted by Steinbrenner who offered his job back if he could manage to get fired from Oakland. Martin obliged by displaying reprehensible behavior, demoting gay players, traveling with his mistress, and trashing his office when the team refused him a loan to pay off tax debts.

- In 1983, the Yankees hired Martin with a long-term contract, but Steinbrenner fired him at the end of the season, moving him to a scouting job. Billy was back in 1985 and managed a second-place finish, but second was not good enough for the impulsive Steinbrenner. Steinbrenner fired Billy as manager but raised his salary (!) keeping him on as an advisor and retiring his number 1(!)

"I may not have been the greatest Yankee to ever put on the uniform, but I was the proudest."

— BILLY MARTIN

- Billy again took the helm in 1988, but off-the-field troubles plagued the dynamic personality.

A brawl in a nightclub, looming marital troubles, and an ejection that led to a suspension for throwing dirt at an umpire contributed to Martin being dismissed halfway through the season. He was again moved to a consultant position marking the eighth time he managed to get fired from his position as manager.

- Penciled-in to manage the Yankees again in 1990 for his sixth tour as manager, the hopes of fans and management were thwarted by Martin's untimely death in a car accident near his home on Christmas day.

"[Martin was] one of the most magnetic, enter-taining, sensitive, humane, brilliant, generous, insecure, paranoid, dangerous, irrational, and unhinged people I had ever met."

— BILL PENNINGTON

Being feisty is not really a prerequisite to being a successful manager. In fact, managers come in all flavors from the silent tacticians to the Napoleonic governors to the masters of chaos. The one thing all great managers seem to possess is a passion and knowledge of the game, a notion that nothing less than winning is acceptable, and a curious ability to inspire players and fans with their passion. Martin's monomaniacal desire to win—especially as a Yankee—drove him to unmatched highs and lows in his career and personal life. But certainly, he is an extreme in the game of baseball.

---

1. Whitey Ford is sometimes included in this story, but it seems unlikely.
2. The validity of the entire story is sometimes questioned because similar tales have been told by comedians, writers, and in the press. It suggests these pranksters may have appropriated the story and adapted it for their own purposes.
3. This clip shows the altercation: https://youtu.be/HHctFAj1ywI

14

DO NOT GO GENTLE INTO THAT GOOD NIGHT

The title name comes from a poem by the Welsh poet Dylan Thomas that is meant to acknowledge that every life ends in death but that should not be a reason to quit. In this case, the use of the title is meant to suggest that a warrior in the game recognizes they have been a champion and do not give in to a slow and dismal fade into obscurity.

Of all the storied careers that seem improbable, impossible, or flat-out lies, there is a rare breed of players who end their careers on a high note—a place where they seem to play their best moments before bowing gracefully into retirement. Mike Mussina's underappreciated eighteen-year career ended with his first twenty-win season at the age of 39, and that achievement probably got him into the Hall of Fame. Ted

Williams came back after a disappointing season in 1959 as if he had something to prove, redeemed his reputation, and walked off the season with his final at-bat being a home run at the age of 41. In that season, he eclipsed the cherished 500 home run pinnacle even though he missed about five years of his prime due to military service. David Ortiz retired in 2016 after hitting a record 38 homers—the highest number by a player in their final season—at the age of 40. Each of these players had all but announced their retirement in their final year. Each achieved commemorable goals.

One far more improbable figure absolutely dominated baseball for a period of just six years. Entering what he acknowledged to himself as his final season at the age of 30, he pitched to his lowest career ERA (1.73), won the most games of any season he played (twenty-seven), and won his final of three Cy Young awards in the years where only one Cy Young was awarded annually. His career started late, ended early, and as a shooting star blazed into the annals of baseball legends battling the demise of his own body which had encumbered him with crippling arthritis. But it was not to happen before he left his mark on the game.

"There are two times in my life the hair on my arms has stood up: The first time I saw the ceiling of the Sistine Chapel and the first time I saw Sandy Koufax throw a fastball."

— AL CAMPANIS, DODGERS' SCOUT

Koufax was not even a baseball star in his early days. Sandy excelled in basketball. He did play baseball but was a position player, gravitating to catching, and was moved to first base. He pitched only four games in his college career and did play well (3–1, 2.81 ERA, 51 Ks in thirty-two innings) but it was hardly the focus of his athletic endeavors.

The eyes of scouts somehow did the improbable and recognized his more unique talents and promising arm. Despite the fact that he could be relatively wild, Koufax threw hard. So hard that in a tryout with the Pirates, Koufax threw a fastball that broke the thumb of Sam Narron (a bullpen pitching coach).

"When he first came up, he couldn't throw a baseball inside the batting cage."

— DUKE SNIDER, HALL OF FAME
CENTER FIELDER

Koufax took a flier and signed with the Dodgers. Because his signing bonus was over $4,000 dollars, the club was required to keep Koufax on the major-league roster for two years. He saw little action during this time and made just as little progress as a player.

"My first two years in the big leagues I did very little except watch... [I] realized [I] was not trained for my job. I pitched four or five sandlot games and four games in college. That was it."

— SANDY KOUFAX

Between 1955 and 1960, Koufax amassed a less-than-stellar record of 36 and 40, never once with an ERA less than 3.00. Then, in the offseason, Koufax came to a sort of realization.

"I really started working out. I started running more. I decided I was really going to find out how good I can be."

— SANDY KOUFAX

From 1961 to 1966, Sandy Koufax struck out more batters than innings pitched. He went 129 and 47. Three times he threw to an ERA of less than 2.00, leading the league in ERA in five straight seasons. He was a perennial all-star for six straight years. Won two consecutive Cy Young awards in his last two. He was in the top two in MVP voting in three of his final four years, winning one nod in 1963, and losing to Willie Mays in 1965 and Roberto Clemente in 1966. In two of three World Series wins as a player, he was twice named MVP for his ability to take the ball and shut down the opposition.

Over those six years, Koufax also threw four no-hitters and a perfect game. He tamed the wildness that plagued his early career and broke out his potential.

"My first recollection of Sandy Koufax is in Vero Beach—his first spring—and it was like 10 o'clock in the morning and Sandy's first pitch went sailing over the backstop landed on the roof of the press room—'clunk'—and it woke up a 65-year-old sportswriter who was in there take a morning nap."

— JACK LANG, SPORTSWRITER

Sandy had to exit the game as a baby-faced player at just 30 years of age because his body took up against him. No more cursed than Gehrig, he faced the reality of life and purposely threw a dominant season that would mark his achievement, feeling the pain of every pitch but coming through as a giant on his field of dreams so he could hold his head up because of his accomplishments. Too many try to push beyond.

"The man who stands alone is the most dominating pitcher I ever saw—without a doubt, and with no equal—Sandy Koufax."

— DON SUTTON, HALL OF FAME
PITCHER

15

WALK-OFF BALK

The balk[1] is part of that breed of unusual baseball rules that even most baseball players don't completely understand. In its simplest definition, it is when a pitcher comes set with his foot on the pitching rubber and makes any motion that interrupts normal delivery with the intent to deceive the runner or batter —intentional or not. This gets complicated by what is considered "legal."[2] The penalty for "deceiving the runner" is that each runner is awarded a base.

It is the only instance in baseball where runners advance on a ball that never comes into play. Not only that, a run can score.

Since about 1900 there have been 22 walk-off balks. The saddest of these walk-offs is probably a game where the Rangers and the Dodgers were dueling to a 0 to 0 shutout on June 18, 2015. Rookie Keone Kela was having a good season and was called on to pitch the ninth inning. He was only into the thirtieth inning of his MLB career when he seemed to hit a little hitch in the road.

He was 3 balls and 2 strikes on Yasmani Grandal and issued a walk on the sixth pitch. Enrique Hernandez pinch-ran for Grandal. Hernandez was not really a threat to steal as he'd never stolen a base in his career, but Kela probably didn't know that as Hernandez was a rookie as well. Kela threw a four-pitch walk to Andre Ethier, checking the runner between the first and second pitch with a pick-off throw to first. It was now first and second.

After a pick-off attempt at second trying to keep Hernandez close to the bag, Kela ran the count to 3 and 1 without Alberto Callaspo offering at anything. Callaspo bunted the fifth pitch foul to run the count to 3 and 2.

The bunt was now out of the equation because there were two strikes, Callaspo swung away and grounded the next pitch to the first baseman who started a 3-6-3 double play advancing Hernandez to third. What a relief that must have been to Kela.

Now with two down, all Kela had to worry about was Jimmy Rollins who was hitting .200 on the season. The first ball was a called strike. The second was a swinging strike. One more strike and the game would go into extra innings. He threw a ball and the count advanced to 1 ball and 2 strikes. He still had the advantage. He pounded the strike zone forcing Rollins to foul off the next two pitches.

Let's just frame the moment. A runner on third who is not a speedster, two outs already in the bag. You are ahead in the count to a batter who hits at the Mendoza-line.[3] Then the game stopped without Kela throwing a pitch. He was called on a balk as he appeared to react to Hernandez breaking down the line. One pitch away from continuing the game into extra innings in very favorable odds, Kela made the blunder of worrying about a man who had little chance to steal anything, much less home.

This is the vicious potential consequence of the balk.[4]

People hold records for balking. Hall of Fame pitcher Steve Carlton finished his career in 1988 but not before being called for 90 balks in his twenty-four-year career. No one else even comes close. Bob Welsh is second all-time with 45—half as many.

Bob Shaw once gave up 5 balks in one game on May 4, 1963. He gave up 2 more balks in his previous start on April 28. Within just two games, he had a total of 7 balks and ended up with a total of just 12 over a career spanning 1,778 innings. Those two days made up 58 percent of the balks he got over a ten-year career. In all, they amounted to remarkably little offensive production. The only run accomplished by balk was in the third inning. After walking Billy Williams leading off, Shaw balked Williams around the bases over the course of several otherwise unproductive outs. In essence, Williams hit a home run just by standing in the batter's box, only he technically never had to take his bat off his shoulder to score. It seems that is a performance that is hard to outdo.

In stepped Jim Gott, August 6, 1988, looking for a challenge.

Relieving in the eighth inning of a game against the Mets with a 3 to 2 lead, Gott threw to pinch-hitter Tim Teufel and walked him on seven pitches. With Dave Magadan at bat, Gott balked sending Teufel to second base, removing the force. Magadan then grounded out on what might have been a double play to the second baseman, but Teufel advanced to third. Darryl Strawberry stepped in and grounded the ball to second. The second baseman threw home and Teufel beat the throw.

It was scored a fielder's choice: the run scored and Strawberry ended up at first. It was a run that scored to tie the game all because the balk took away the force for the double play.

Kevin McReynolds ran the count to 2 balls and 0 strikes before taking the third pitch to right-center for a double. It was second and third with just one out. Gary Carter took his turn at the plate and just stood there. Gott didn't even get off a pitch to Carter and balked to score Strawberry. The Mets took a 4 to 3 lead. McReynolds, also awarded a base, went to third. Carter walked on five pitches, actually swinging and fouling off the second pitch. Howard Johnson struck out swinging on just three pitches. Kevin Elster stepped up with two out with runners on first and third, and on a 2 ball 1 strike count just stood there as Gott balked for the third time in the inning. This scored McReynolds and sent Carter to second base. The Mets scored three runs, arguable all because of balks and they led the Pirates 5 to 3. Mackey Sasser pinch-hit for Bob McClure, the Pirates relieved Gott with Jeff Robinson who got Sasser to ground out 6–3 to end what is probably the inning most influenced by balks in the history of baseball. The Pirates went on to lose the game 3 to 5, with Gott taking the loss, having given up 1 hit, 3 walks, 3 balks, and 3 runs in two-thirds of an inning. Gott had 6 balks on the year in 1988, and in

1,170 innings as a big-league player, committed only 15 balks.

Certainly, the 22 walk-off balks were heart-breaking ways to lose games, but not one of those performances balked a man around the bases or scored three runs for the opposing team. They all just brought in a final run when a game was tied and did not contribute to the tying, go-ahead, and insurance runs that a team needed to win a game.

Three balks, one inning, three runs in. That is the ultimate in mechanical despair.

---

1. See the official baseball rules section 6.02(a) for a complete discussion of the definition of a balk.
   https://content.mlb.com/documents/2/2/4/305750224/
   2019_Official_Baseball_Rules_FINAL_.pdf.
2. Until 2013, pitchers were allowed to fake a throw toward third and spin to throw toward first or second, occupied or not.
3. Typically referred to as .200, or 1 in 5 chance of success.
4. The box score shows every step of the event.
   https://www.baseball-reference.com/boxes/LAN/
   LAN201506180.shtml

16

SUPER JOE

Players remembered in baseball lore often remain there because of their antics off the field as much as the achievements on it. A sad and strange corner of baseball is the group of shooting stars who really were great players but often had their careers cut short. The fans of the game are left to wonder "what if..."

In this category, you find players like Mark Fidrych, a phenom in his first year at the age of 21 in 1976. He went 19 and 9 that year not at all depending on striking out batters,[1] instead relying on his relationship with the baseball. Watching him on the mound, it seemed Fidrych was coaxing the ball to do his will by talking to it. He played as if he were a condensed cartoon version of Zack Greinke, apparently doing more to freak out batters than dominate them. Fidrych was named "The

Bird" after the goofy, gigantic feathered character named Big Bird on the long-running children's program Sesame Street.[2] Fidrych drew fans by the tens of thousands to ballparks across the league with his on-field dynamic.

Pete Reiser, another unique character, never met a cement or brick wall without serious injury. He played the game with an aggressiveness and skill somewhere between Pete Rose, Shoeless Joe Jackson, and Ty Cobb and is considered by some as one of the greatest baseball players of all time. His downfall was his enthusiasm. Ebbets Field was the first ballpark in the major leagues with padded walls and they were installed because of the insane way Reiser went after fly balls. He was taken off the field on a stretcher a record eleven times. That is a stat that does not make the box score and it is probably ten more times than any other player in MLB history. On June 4, 1947, Reiser was administered last rites after a collision with a wall. He was credited with the catch.[3]

As sensational and yet obscure as these players were, another appeared on the radar for a total of 647 at-bats over 201 games in the early '80s. That's the 1980s. That needs to be clarified because parts of his story seem to be from another era. He was touted as a tough-as-nails type of player who hit for power and average, and did manage to set a record: least games played by a position player after being voted Rookie of the Year.[4] After the 1980 season, he appeared in only seventy more games as his career was derailed by a back injury from which he never fully recovered. Regardless of the brevity of his career, Joe Charboneau managed to make a lasting impression on fans. His first hit, in his first game and second at-bat in the majors, was a home run. Like any true mythical hero, he had a song written about him.[5]

"Almost immediately, I realized there was something about him. He emanated greatness. I really think he was born to be great."

— JOE NOSSEK, AN INDIANS' COACH

As a boy, Joe had trouble sitting still and had trouble not getting into trouble. He likely had undiagnosed ADHD, like Rube Waddell. Eventually, his energy, academic indifference, and other challenges led him to be declared ineligible to play baseball—the one thing he seemed to settle into with some direction and success. This didn't turn out to be an improvement because he found other—less productive—ways to channel his energy. This is how the legend of "Super Joe" Charboneau[6] was born.

During his exile from organized ball at school, Joe sought adventure. He took on odd challenges such as taking part in bare-knuckle boxing matches to earn some extra money. He got $25 for a win and $15 for a loss, but $5 went to the person who set up the match. These were not proper bare-knuckle matches. Everything was legal except for weapons. He lost more than he won, had his nose broken several times, and once tried to fix his wrinkled schnozz with a pair of pliers. He must have been somewhat impervious to pain, as he admitted to pulling his own tooth with a vice grip and cutting off a tattoo he got with a razor when he decided he didn't like it.

Trouble followed Joe into the streets, and he also got into fights with people who were not fighting for money. He claimed to have been stabbed three times in these less lucrative bouts and once closed a wound on his own using fishing line. Later when with the Indians for exhibition games in Mexico City, Joe was approached by a fellow who seemed to be looking for an autograph, pen in hand. The man asked Joe where he was from and when Joe answered, Oscar Martinez —who hated Americans—drove his pen into Joe's side, plunging it in four inches. Martinez was caught and fined 50 pesos. That was the equivalent of about $2.27.

In the days of the minors, he was exposed to other players' antics and took dares like swallowing whole eggs—shell on—which he did once. It lodged in his throat and he began choking when a quick-thinking friend punched him in the egg and it broke up so he could swallow it. He somehow found out that he could drink beer through his repaired nose. He won a $25 bet by eating six lit cigarettes. He bought himself a pet alligator with distinct aspirations, named the gator Chopper, and kept it in his bathtub.[7]

"I was going to train him to wrestle me. He would have grown to be about six feet long, so I would have had the height advantage."

— JOE CHARBONEAU

It became impractical to move Chopper when Joe switched teams, so he left the animal in the care of a teammate. During that time Chopper attempted to escape and fatally injured himself in the process. The alligator is supposedly the reason for a curse that has fallen over the team.

Like many of the pranksters, jokesters, and mythical heroes of the game, Joe's fabled history followed him and people attributed things to his history that were not his own. Some claimed he had his own vaudeville show and said they'd seen him eat lightbulbs and shot glasses. But one thing is certain: he played well enough in minor league ball to be called up in 1980.

"Making it to the big leagues was the highlight for me. Baseball was good back then. You played for the love of the game and you didn't make a lot of money. There were fewer teams and better pitching. It was harder to make it."

— JOE CHARBONEAU

In Joe's first home game, April 19, Joe went 3 for 3 with a home run, a double, and a walk immediately capturing the attention and imagination of the fans. Later that season, on June 28, Joe hit what is considered to be one of the three longest home runs ever hit in Yankee Stadium achieving what storied Yankee sluggers such as Mantle, the Babe, Gehrig, Maris, and DiMaggio never did.

As the antics and actualities began to mount, Joe became a hero in the city of Cleveland. By mid-season, a song was released featuring Joe and the locals ate up the 45 single. It rose to number four on the charts. Cleveland may not be a big town to win over, but the fanatical fans helped push his fame to greater heights and he ended up on magazine covers and TV shows. Joe found it hard to believe this was happening to him.

When the season came to a close, Charboneau seemed headed for a career with the mega-stars of the sport. But fortunes turned in spring training when Joe injured his back during a head-first slide. He tried to play through it, but his regression at the plate sent him back to the minors. Things did not improve much, and while Joe surfaced a few times over the next few seasons, he was not invited to stay. On June 1, 1982, with his batting average at .214, he left major league baseball for the final time. From there he went to the Buffalo affiliate and was released in 1983.

> "Well, maybe this is it. I've had my year and a half in the big leagues. Maybe that's all I've got coming."
>
> — JOE CHARBONEAU TO A REPORTER
> AS HE EMPTIED HIS LOCKER

Joe may have no longer had a playing career, but he did have a legend, and that lived on past the end of his career. He made appearances and got to enjoy the power of the myth and legend built around his time in the big leagues.

1. Fidrych had only 97 Ks in 250 innings.
2. Sesame Street originally aired in 1969 and still runs on public television as educational programming for young kids.
3. Gene Hermanski admitted much later to putting the ball in Reiser's glove as Reiser lay motionless so he would be credited with the catch.
4. From Bob Bloss's book *Rookies of the Year* (2005). Mark Fidrych only appeared in twenty-seven games after his rookie year, but he was a pitcher.
5. "Go Joe Charboneau" by Section 36. https://youtu.be/S2JV0btxRvQ
6. His name is sometimes misspelled Charbonneau, which is a more common spelling and is confused with a Canadian Archbishop.
7. This is disputed in *Crazy, with the Papers to Prove It*, by Dan Coughlin. He does say Joe acquired the pet, but that he also purchased a $300 aquarium to keep it in.

17

YOU THROW LIKE A GIRL

When I was a kid, I was lucky enough to live next door to a guy who loved baseball. He was a tough construction worker, had a grizzly voice, chain-smoked Lucky Strikes, and spent most of his time in a t-shirt. He and his wife were never able to have children, so Rocco took me and my brothers under his wing to teach us how to play ball. He was no pro, but we learned tons about the game before we were old enough to play it seriously ourselves. He was great at encouraging us. Getting started throwing early made sure I'd never throw like a girl.

Later when I had my first kid, I couldn't wait to have a catch. I probably started way too early, but the result was that she never threw like a girl either. Yeah, she was a girl, but she never threw like one.

Looking back, I'm sure it was because she started at an early age. The mechanics of "throwing like a girl" were really just a myth.[1] The reality is that girls aren't encouraged to throw or play baseball so they don't develop those skills and muscle memory. They don't learn to leverage the torque of their torso and, because of that, their elbow dominates the throw making it look weak rather than throwing from the shoulder.

Now consider growing up next door to a Hall of Fame pitcher, let's say Dazzy Vance, who led the league in strikeouts seven times in a career that spanned twenty years.[2] Imagine he took you under his wing and taught you how to throw his famous "drop pitch." Chances are that even if you were a girl, you wouldn't end up throwing like one.

Joe Engel built Engel Stadium in 1930 to be the home of the Washington Senators' first minor league affiliate, the Chattanooga Lookouts. Over the years that followed, Engel became known as the "Barnum of the Bushes"[3]—the minor league version of Bill Veeck[4] who chose to host baseball games as promotional events to draw in the fans and the sparse dollars of depression-era crowds. He had his players parade onto the field on elephants for opening day,[5] distributed canaries in cages around the park, traded a player for a turkey,[6] reenacted Custer's last stand,[7] raffled off a house to attending fans (cramming more than 25,000 attendees into a stadium that held 12,000), and hired a woman to play pro ball.

"I don't care what you say about me, as long as you say something."[8]

— JOE ENGEL

Engel was a successful scout who is credited with discovering Babe Ruth and Joe Cronin, amongst other players. On March 25, 1931, Engel scouted and signed Jackie Mitchell, a 17-year-old girl because he saw a promotional opportunity. She was a girl and an incorrigible tomboy whose father started her playing baseball from a young age. Their neighbor, Dazzy Vance, helped to coach her in throwing a ball.

Engel's Chattanooga Lookouts were scheduled for two exhibition games against the New York Yankees, whose lineup still sported both Babe Ruth and Lou Gehrig. The first game, originally scheduled for April 1,[9] was rained out. The next day, Jackie did not start the game, but after the starting pitcher let up a double and a run-scoring single, the coach put Jackie in to face Babe Ruth.

Ruth took the first pitch for a ball. Film of the at-bat shows Ruth swinging and missing on the second and third pitch to make the count 1 ball and 2 strikes.[10] Ruth stepped in and took a called strike on the outside of the plate. He threw his bat down after the call, seemingly in disgust with the umpire. Gehrig got up and struck out swinging at three straight pitches. Tony Lazzari then walked on five pitches and Mitchell was lifted from the game and replaced with the starting pitcher.

While neither Ruth nor Gehrig ever admitted to the strikeouts being staged, they never fully denied it either. While opinions vary, Engel himself let on that it was a ruse in a letter to the press in 1955.

"She couldn't pitch hay to a cow."

— JOE ENGEL

Mitchell, either misinformed of the reality of her appearance or refusing to let on that she was in on the gag, insisted until her death in 1987 that the strikeouts were no joke.

"Why, hell yes, [Ruth and Gehrig] were trying, damn right. Hell, better hitters than them couldn't hit me. Why should they've been any different?"[11]

— JACKIE MITCHELL

Just days after Jackie's appearance, baseball Commissioner, Kenesaw Mountain Landis, voided her contract, essentially banning her from playing baseball. She continued to play in barnstorming games and participated in crowd-pleasing promotional events like riding onto the field on a donkey,[12] but eventually put baseball aside to work at her father's optician's shop.

Jackie's appearance against these great players may have been a burlesque of sorts in the era of vaudeville and the Great Depression, but it should stand as a question as to whether there is really such a thing as "throwing like a girl." A girl can only throw like a girl because they have no other choice. But if that girl can strike out some of the greatest hitters in a game, maybe someday we will see a female player start in the major leagues.

---

1. This is verified to a great extent in an episode of the MythBusters TV program where they take an in-depth look at what it means to "throw like a girl." https://youtu.be/LD5Xm5u7UDM

2. Vance's career spanned twenty years, but he was injured early on and missed several years before suddenly regaining his form at the age of 31 after having bone chips removed from his shoulder. He then came back gangbusters to lead the league in strikeouts for seven straight years between 1922 and 1928.

3. "Bushes" refers to bush leagues.

4. Veeck was the famous baseball promoter who did many outrageous things, including hiring a little person to pinch hit (Eddie Gaedel); allowing fans to vote on key decisions during a game("Grandstand Manager's Night"); "Disco Demolition Night" where fans were encouraged to bring unwanted disco albums to the stadium to be demolished by explosives (this drew more than baseball fans and forced the forfeiture of the second game of a double-header); and hiring Max Patkin "the Clown Prince of Baseball" to coach, effectively distracting fans and players with his antics from the coaching box.

5. It is not clear from varied accounts whether these elephants were real or papier-mâché, whether there was a parade or an elephant hunt, or whether two different events are merged in accounts of the event(s).

6. Johnny "Binky" Jones whose career MLB stats include 25 hits and 8 walks in sixteen-and-a-third innings while picking up a win.

7. Custer won in Engel's version.

8. "Obituaries," The Sporting News, June 13, 1969: 44.

9. There arises some controversy over whether the whole event was staged as an April Fool's joke because of the original date.

10. https://www.smithsonianmag.com/videos/category/history/the-girl-who-struck-out-babe-ruth/ Skip to 4:42 for the video of Ruth striking out.
11. She said this in an interview with a reporter in 1986 for an article in *Smithsonian Magazine*.
12. Donkey baseball was not really played like this farcical account https://youtu.be/HcNWfcdEJ6E

18

A CATASTROPHIC TIE GAME

How many plays in baseball result in suicide? What does it feel like when you end your career and you have to worry that when you die your gravestone will read: "He was a bonehead"?

Players are sometimes remembered for one career-defining play, and for all the wrong reasons. Bill Buckner had a solid twenty-two-year career and instead of being remembered for his consistency and longevity, he is remembered for a play—a single play— in the 1986 World Series that turned the tide in the favor of the New York Mets. He actually botched more than that one in the series, but at the time he performed the career-defining play, the second botch was no longer critical. It was just bad.

In the top of the tenth in that sixth game with a 3 to 2 lead in wins, the Mets had come from a 3 to 0 deficit to tie in the bottom of the eighth, the Red Sox scored two runs. With a 5 to 3 lead, they looked like they were about to walk off the field as World Champions, dousing the "Curse of the Bambino."[1] With two out in the bottom of the tenth, trailing by two, Met's Hall of Fame catcher, Gary Carter, singled. Kevin Mitchell came in to pinch-hit, and he singled to make it first-and-second. On a 0 and 2 count, the Mets down to their last strike, Ray Knight hit a single scoring Carter and leaving it first and third with two out. Mookie Wilson came up, and in the course of a ten pitch at-bat, he induced a wild pitch to tie the game on the seventh pitch. Three pitches later, he hit one of the most famous ground balls ever. It looked like an easy out to send the game to the eleventh inning, but it went through the wickets of Bill Buckner's legs. Knight was flying with two out and no one could retrieve the ball in time.

Knight Scored the winning and brought them to game 7 where they became world champions. It was a mistake a veteran should not have made, but being on the national stage, his disgrace was broadcast and marked him forever.

Fred Merkle was a 19-year-old kid in 1908 playing in his second season with the New York Giants. In a game on September 23 of that year, he had not yet had one hundred plate appearances and had never started a game until that day, playing backup to the team's starting first baseman, Fred Tenney.[2] Merkle was called on to start as Tenney woke up with low back pain. He walked once in four plate appearances and then, in the bottom of the ninth inning, Merkle came to bat with two outs, a man on first, and the score tied 1 to 1.

Merkle singled and McCormick advanced to third base. Al Bridwell followed Merkle with another single, scoring McCormick with what should have been the winning run. Fans flooded the field thinking that the game was over because they just saw the winning run cross home plate. But Merkle, possibly confused by the stampede, turned and ran to the Giants' clubhouse without touching second base. He forgot that he was still required to touch second before leaving the field because he was the lead runner in a force play.

Johnny Evers was a shrewd veteran in his seventh year in the big leagues. He noticed Merkle failed to touch second. He retrieved a ball,[3] touched second base, and appealed to the umpire. The ump called Merkle out. As the third out was made, the run did not score and the game remained a tie. With the chaos of thousands of fans on the field and with night coming on, the game was called off and the umpires declared it a tie.

As fate would have it, the Giants and the Cubs ended the season tied for first place. It appeared that the game that they tied had to be replayed to determine who came in first. The Cubs took the makeup game, 4 to 2 ending the season for the Giants. Then the Cubs went on to win the World Series that year in five games over the Tigers.

Harry Pulliam was the President of the National League at the time of incidents that found the Cubs and Giants in a tie at the end of the season. After "Merkle's Boner,"[4] Pulliam reviewed the decision of the umpires and agreed with them, never expecting that the game would end up being critical to the pennant race. When the tie resulted from regular play, the National League Council held a special meeting to again review the play. They upheld Pulliam's earlier decision, and in a report went on to berate Merkle for his "reckless, careless, inexcusable blunder."[5]

As anyone might expect, Merkle was distraught over his role in the events. When his playing career ended, he moved on from baseball and did not look back for twenty-four years. In 1950 at the age of 62, Merkle accepted an invitation to the Giant's Old-Timers' Day. The kind crowd welcomed him with a standing ovation. Fred died five years later of natural causes. His hometown of Watertown, Wisconsin, has several commemorations raised for Merkle.

While one might expect Merkle to be the one most affected by the events and the weight of his blunder, Harry Pulliam was perhaps more deeply troubled. He took off several months after the end of the season and was noted by acquaintances to have become particularly moody. On September 28, 1909, Pulliam was found shot in his room at the New York Athletic Club. The shooting appeared to have been an attempted suicide, and the damage was great. It did not immediately kill him, though the bullet passed completely through his skull from temple to temple, blinding him. The doctor in attendance asked Pulliam what the reason for the shooting was, and Pulliam answered: "Who is shot? I am not shot." He then became unconscious and never regained consciousness again.

There are many theories about the reason for the suicide that go beyond the idea that Pulliam's state of depression was only due to Merkle's Boner to include the saucy state of affairs in the political battles within the league. Some theories even suggest Pulliam may have been murdered. It is, of course, unlikely that the true story will come to light.

---

1. The "curse" had to do with selling Babe Ruth to the New York Yankees. Supposedly, the sale had to do with the owner of the Sox wanting to finance Broadway shows, including *"No, No, Nanette."* To that point (1920) Boston had been a dominant force in baseball. Ruth went for $125,000 dollars ($1,728,681.25 dollars in 2021, see https://www.in2013dollars.com/us/inflation/1920?amount=125000).

2. Merkle's total plate appearances were 91 at the moment of the incident.

3. It is hard to tell if the ball he retrieved was the game ball or not, as accounts differ.

4. The event actually left Merkle with a playing error named after him.

5. "Cubs and Giants to Play Off Tie," *Chicago Tribune*, October 7, 1908.

19

THE SOUND OF SILENT DOMINANCE

Most superstars are remembered for the things they do with a bat or the prowess of their arm. Some are known for aggressive play, foolish antics, personalities, and moments that became larger than life. But there are players who forge long careers in a sort of quiet persistence, not known for anything but their glove. When you are in a game as a rookie and you hit the first home run of your career in the same game that Mickey Mantle hits the 500th of his career, nobody knows your name. Especially when that will be the first of only twenty home runs in an eighteen-year career to go with a lifetime batting average of .228 and slugging percentage of .280. Those are not typos. He holds the dubious honor of being the player who was pinch-hit for the most in history (333).

> "There is no such thing as good pitching without good defense."
>
> — SANDY KOUFAX

For a glove-first player to hold real value for a team, they can't just be good at what they do. They have to be the best. These are players who have a fine work ethic and probably nothing short of obsession with the mechanics of playing the field. Their style of play may be sharp and seemingly effortless but it will lack sparkle. In fact, it might be downright dull. Take that player and his eight Gold Gloves and stick him between a third baseman who won sixteen straight Gold Gloves,[1] and two different second basemen who won a total of seven over eight seasons,[2] and there is a defensive dynasty. It is how you come to have four starting pitchers on one team winning twenty games each in the same year. It is hard to believe that situation was just because those players happened to play with one another. It seems more likely that they held each other in esteem, and sometimes held each other up.

"I never ever saw him blow a routine play. [Blade][3] had wonderful range... He was special out there."

— BOOG POWELL, *100 THINGS ORIOLES FANS SHOULD KNOW & DO BEFORE THEY DIE* BY DAN CONNOLLY

Mark "Blade" Belanger is not a player most people will know unless they are a fan of the Orioles or followed baseball in the '70s. He is also particularly difficult to profile because extensive defensive metrics were not the stats of his day. He ranged in the shadow of probably the greatest fielding third baseman ever to play the game on teams where big bats, great arms, and diving catches grabbed the headlines. Somehow Belanger, although a great athlete, seemed to effortlessly cover the ground he defended and was always just where he needed to be.

"Belanger would glide effortlessly after a grounder and welcome it into loving arms; scooping the ball up with a single easy motion, and bringing it to his chest for a moment's caress before making his throw."

— PAT JORDAN, "YEARS AHEAD OF HIS TIME," *SPORTS ILLUSTRATED*, JULY 29, 1974

The combination of style and smarts gave Belanger some power over the outcome of the game. He shared that as a team player, teaching what he knew to younger guys on the way up seemingly unconcerned that they might be there for his job. He helped create a practically impenetrable wall of defense that made pitchers better at what they did.

"[Trying to get a hit through the left side of the Baltimore infield is like] trying to throw a hamburger through a brick wall."

— DETROIT TIGERS' MANAGER, MAYO SMITH

One way to see in the mind's eye how Belanger worked is to look at his actions in a complicated play. He was involved in one of the most exotic triple plays in baseball where he let up a run but saved the game. Triple plays are strange enough because you have to have certain conditions. There have to be no outs with two runners on base. That immediately makes it much more rare than a double play. Generally, the ball in a triple play will have the first out made in the infield.

On June 3, 1977, Belanger was playing short in a game against the Royals. It was the often fabled bottom of the ninth inning and the Royals were down 7 to 5. Two innings earlier Belanger sent a fly ball to left field to score an insurance run on a sacrifice fly—which it turns out to be a run the Orioles would need. Al Cowens led off the inning with a double, Dave Nelson walked, and then Freddie Patek hit a single to load the bases. Tippy Martinez who was usually bank for the Orioles just wasn't getting it done. The O's still had a two-run lead, but Kansas City had three outs to inflict some damage with the winning run already on base.

John Wathen pinch-hit with his average at a whopping .417. Wathen hit a fly ball to right field that Pat Kelly caught, but all the runners were tagging up to create some chaos on the base paths. Cowens scored easily after the catch. Kelly threw to Belanger who caught

Freddie Patek by feeding the ball to Billy Smith at second who got the ball back to Belanger who tagged out Patek. Dave Nelson skidded off to third base, deciding to try to score seeing the run-down and not expecting it to go so easily. Belanger saw Nelson make the turn and ran at him as he was halfway down the line. Nelson had to choose a direction and headed toward home. Belanger tagged him out ten feet from home plate and the inning was over.

Belanger commandeered the whole mess, masterfully dissecting the play as it unfolded and neatly clearing the base paths for another day. He just didn't do it loudly enough to make the Hall of Fame.

"The guy had the greatest glove at shortstop I've ever seen. He just didn't have the batting average... Damn right, he's in my Hall of Fame. Blade and Brooksie made me a Hall of Famer."

— JIM PALMER

---

1. Brooks Robinson, 1960 to 1975.
2. Davey Johnson, 1969 to 1971; Bobby Grich, 1973 to 1976.
3. Mark Belanger's nickname.

20

THE SPACEMAN WHO WAS
IMPERVIOUS TO BUS FUMES

If Zack Greinke had a forefather in the baseball realm, it was probably Bill Lee. They do look a little alike if you compare them at similar ages. Lee didn't quite dominate in his day like Greinke has but he had his moments and was a competitor. Lee was certainly more outspoken and willing to share his views in a way that is practically opposite to Greinke. The fact that he readily shared his views is exactly what earned him the nickname "Spaceman." He embraced his ideals and accepted uncommon and unpopular world views that may be seen as peculiar by people more conservatively rooted. But if you really consider his words, you have to also consider who is crazy.

> "I'm mad at Hank (Aaron) for deciding to play
> one more season. I threw him his last home
> run and thought I'd be remembered forever.
> Now, I'll have to throw him another."[1]
>
> — BILL "SPACEMAN" LEE

It is exactly through these perspectives that you get to know the skewed view of the man and how the skew makes sense. He is not really just some raving lunatic (although he admits to having his moments of tossing garbage pails and breaking chairs), but he does believe in the ideals of enjoying life and revels in history and nostalgia. That really isn't such a crazy thing. if you think about it.

"I love watching the older games and the guys with full windups. These guys are out there and they play baseball. They never pulled muscles. They never had weight machines. They never did stretching. They played pepper, they chewed tobacco, and they went and played baseball. They had a good time [and when] the game was over and they went out had a couple of brews, went home, and did it again."[2]

— BILL LEE

Spaceman was traded from Boston to Montreal after Lee continually had questions with Don Zimmer's handling of the pitching staff. Later, Lee was released from the Expos when he staged a walkout in protest of the Expos releasing Rodney Scott. He was essentially black-balled at that point and couldn't peddle his services to other major league teams. From that vantage, it seemed that Lee became even more comfortable with looking back at his career. One thing was clear, he wasn't very interested in rules.

> "[I cheated] every chance I could get. You couldn't chew slippery elm[3] anymore... a lot of spitballers threw... You put a little pine tar on your thumb to get more friction on the bottom of the ball, then you put slippery elm on the top [of the ball] and then you have a tumbling fastball that [batters] just can't flat out hit. Man! If you can make the ball go down and you can only hit the top half of the ball... you don't need any outfielders you can take them and just put them on the bench... most hitters are dumber than a post, so they'll never make [an] adjustment. I love sinkers. I love spitballs. I love anything will make the ball go downward..."[4]
>
> — BILL LEE

What most people see in Lee's words is not the humor, but the horror of how it grates against their modern reality. His attitude is generally one of loving fun, life, nature, and baseball. It was meant to be a game that you play hard to compete and win, and it turned into a business that broke with the spirit of the game.

"Baseball is timeless. You play it on beautiful fields when the grass turns green. You don't play when it rains. Baseball is a civilized game without a clock."[5]

— BILL LEE

In 1988, the Spaceman decided to run for president as the Rhino Party candidate. The party's spirit was inspired by an election in Brazil in the 1950s, where dissatisfied citizens nominated and subsequently elected a hippopotamus to a municipal post. Jacques Ferron founded the Rhino Party in 1963 choosing a rhinoceros as a symbol of being thick-skinned, stupid, and myopic while loving to wallow in the mud. One of the more famed platform policies was to lower the boiling point of water to save energy. They believed in bulldozing the Rocky Mountains so Eastern parts of Canada would get more sunlight.

"I don't like working. I like to play. And any day you're not in the sawmill or you're not in the woods cutting trees, and you're on a ball field you live a little longer. So I try to play as much baseball as I can."

— BILL LEE

In the book *The Wrong Stuff*,[6] an oft-maligned pitch about using marijuana suggested to many people that he was a frequent substance abuser. Combined with Lee's interesting perspectives, the idea of being heavily involved in drug culture explained his perspectives and behaviors. Lee never really denies marijuana use. It got him in some trouble with the commissioner, Bowie Kuhn. In an appearance on *Late Night with David Letterman*, Spaceman recalled the phone call he had with Kuhn.

"The headline said I smoked it. I didn't say I "smoked." I said I "used it"... I [told him I] put it on my pancakes... I'd eat them and run five miles to the ballpark and it makes me impervious to the bus fumes. He says: 'Well I think I could buy that.' And I said: 'Would you like to buy a bridge?"[7]

— BILL LEE

The curious follow-up was that Letterman asked Lee if he smoked marijuana or used it on his pancakes, Lee quickly denied that. When questioned further as to if he ever tried it, Lee admits to having tried it many times. True to form he creates a smokescreen for the truth where you are left between the dichotomy of his two worlds.

"My best pitch is a strike."[8]

— BILL LEE

"People are too hung up on winning. I can get off on a really good helmet throw."[9]

— BILL LEE

Exploring the words and worlds of Bill Lee is one that seems more of a labyrinth of interest and passion for the love of life, living, and baseball than a dive into madness. The craziest ones are those who can't play a game and have fun. This chapter would be misrepresented with anything other than the weight of his own words.

"I want real beer, real hot dogs, real whole wheat buns and that's what baseball is. Baseball is this field of dreams. It's you with your father playing catch... fielding ground balls... [and] never making an error."

— BILL LEE

1. On September 14, 1975, Bill Lee did throw Hank Aaron what would have been his final HR if Aaron had retired at the end of the

year. Instead Dick Drago owns the badge of having given up Aaron's final homer on June 20, 1976.

2. A great interview on NPR with Bill Lee, *Fresh Air with Dave Davies*, February 28, 2005.

   https://www.npr.org/player/embed/4516268/4516269

3. Slippery elm bark is known to increase saliva and is usually used to help reduce throat irritation.

4. Also from *Fresh Air with Dave Davies*, February 28, 2005.

5. When an interview is good, you use it. *Fresh Air with Dave Davies*, February 28, 2005.

6. The first of four books Lee co-wrote about his adventures.

7. Bill Lee's appearance on Letterman: https://youtu.be/jeKwtn8r0FU?t=746

8. Interview: https://youtu.be/g1Bmr8hoCkg

9. Michael Gershman, *The Baseball Card Engagement Book*, 1990.

21

YOU ARE BETTER WHEN YOU PITCH A LITTLE HUNGOVER

The title of this chapter is influenced by the subject of the previous chapter. Bill Lee, in talking about the brief part of his career that criss-crossed with Juan Marichal in Boston in 1974, said Marichal suggested to Lee that it was better to pitch a little hungover. The idea was not really that being hungover improved motor skills, but it spurred a competitive advantage because it forced you to concentrate more on what you were doing. You could not simply walk up and use your given skills.

It seems that, just like PEDs, alcohol has those players it favors the fortunes of and those who it takes from the game. Hack Wilson is a tragic case who fell from the height of success hitting 56 HRs, .356, with 191 RBI[1] that year while carousing at the peak of his powers. He carried that behavior into the offseason, reported to camp 20 pounds heavier, and sank into his demise. Later he lamented his downfall and what might have been had he paid more attention to his health.

Paul Waner believed that he was a better player when intoxicated, but that would be hard to prove with any certainty. After all, we all sing better after a few glasses of wine at the karaoke bar. Waner really thought that drinking gave him an advantage and believed that its magic was the key to his success as a hitter.

"When I walked up there with a half-pint of whiskey fresh in my gut, that ball came in looking like a basketball. But if I hadn't downed my half-pint of 100 proof, that ball came in like an aspirin tablet."

— PAUL WANER

Contemporaries were aware of his tendencies and were only left to tolerate them because they could not disprove the result.

"Paul Waner had to be a very graceful player because he could slide without breaking the bottle on his hip."

— CASEY STENGEL

"Paul Waner, when he was sober, was the best right fielder the Pirates ever had. The second best right fielder the Pirates ever had was Paul Waner when he was drunk."

— JOE TRONZO, SPORTS EDITOR,
THE NEWS-TRIBUNE, BEAVER FALLS,
PA (1971)

There is one strange and rare achievement that two pitchers have admitted to in modern-day ball that seems to outdo even Dock Ellis' no-no. David Wells, a player never known to shy away from carousing, and Dallas Braden were both able to pitch perfect games while drunk, hungover, or a combination of these. The course of their careers would go in quite different directions.

Wells pitched the perfect game on Sunday, May 17, 1998. Wells was known to hang out with some of the cast of Saturday Night Live[2] in the after-parties when the show was done taping. The season for the show had ended,[3] but part of the group met up anyway. Wells did not make his way home until around 5.30 a.m., and he did not have much time to sleep before getting up to go to his scheduled start on Sunday. He arrived at the ballpark a wreck. He described his condition as still being half-drunk with monster breath and a raging, skull-rattling hangover. It was Beanie Baby Day at the stadium and the promotion attracted a full stadium and a buzz in the crowd.

When Wells went to warm up for the game, he claims he had the worst bullpen session of his career. It was so bad he just stopped throwing.

"A lot of times when I had good bullpens, I'd feel invincible and try to be too fine, and then don't last two innings. When you get out there and you're too fine, a lot of things can go wrong."

— DAVID WELLS

Possibly because of something similar to Juan Marichal's logic, Wells got into the game and started mowing down Twins. About halfway through the game, Yankee announcers started doing the unthinkable and mentioning that Wells was pitching a perfect game. His friend and teammate tried to keep Wells in spirits of the non-liquored kind and distracted him from his performance.

"You got nothin'. You're a pussy if you don't show 'em a knuckleball."

— DAVID CONE

Wells didn't throw a knuckleball. But the words from his friend might have been just the thing to get him through the game. About three hours after it started, it was over, and Wells had pitched only the fifteenth perfect game in baseball history to that date. Wells went on to pitch for another seven solid years before his inning count began to fall. He almost pitched another perfect game that season on September 1, but Jason Giambi broke it up in the seventh inning with a single. He faced only two more batters than the minimum.

Dallas Braden's perfect game hangover came on May 9, 2010. He was not so much casually celebrating like Wells did, as lamenting the loss of his mother some years before on the eve of Mother's Day. The next day, his start was 1 p.m., and his grandmother beat him to the stadium.

"There was zero of my usual preparation. Until that day, I had never treated a start or the day before a start the way I did that day. I was [not] telling myself, 'Let's get crushed and tomorrow will be awesome.' It was more like, 'Let's just forget about tomorrow."[4]

— DALLAS BRADEN

Braden "got through" his perfect game and went on to pitch another twenty-three games that season to no great success, throwing one other 4-hit shutout and a 1-hit (eight-inning) appearance. But less than a year after his perfect game, he was on his way out of the major leagues.

It is impossible to really know if any of the other perfect games were pitched under the influence or how a player's behavior leading up to a game affected their performance. But there may be something to the sage words of Juan Marichal who seemed to believe that increasing the challenge can enhance focus. It might not be the right medicine for everyone, but apparently, it works for a select few.

"They say some of my stars drink whiskey. But I have found that the ones who drink milk-shakes don't win many ball games."

— FRED MCMANE

---

1. Wilson's numbers were recognized as deserving of MVP, but the financial stresses of the depression were taking their toll on baseball and no official MVP was named in 1930.
2. NBC's Emmy Award-winning, long-running late-night comedy showcase.
3. Many articles get this wrong. The SNL season for the program ended the week before as Marci Klein confirms.
   https://www.complex.com/sports/2017/05/oral-history-hungover-david-wells-unlikely-perfect-game
4. Quoted from:
   https://www.sfchronicle.com/athletics/article/Dallas-Braden-comes-clean-A-s-starter-was-hung-15251241.php

22

ONE ARM IN THE OUTFIELD

A curious rule change became part of baseball because of a minor league baseball game on June 19, 2008. It was between the Staten Island Yankees and the Brooklyn Cyclones. It was the bottom of the ninth with two out and a runner on first. Staten Island was leading 7 to 2. Ralph Henriquez stepped into the batter's box as a right-hand hitter and Pat Venditte put his glove on his left hand. Henriquez was a switch hitter and moved to the opposite side of the plate to bat left-handed. When he did so, Venditte took off his glove and put it on his right hand to pitch as a lefty. Henriquez stepped to the opposite side of the plate to bat right-handed.

Noticing that this might go on forever and instead of perpetuating the comedy skit, the umpires stepped in to make a decision. After conferring, they decided Henriquez was required to choose a side and remain there. He chose to stand in right-handed. Venditte chose to pitch as a right-hander to leverage the righty-righty match-up and struck out Henriquez on four pitches.

There were rules at the time for similar situations in 8.01(f), 6.06(b), and 6.02(b), but the situation was not fully covered. As such, rule 5.07(f) was added to the official rules.

"A pitcher must indicate visually to the umpire-in-chief, the batter and any runners the hand with which he intends to pitch, which may be done by wearing his glove on the other hand while touching the pitcher's plate. The pitcher is not permitted to pitch with the other hand until the batter is retired, the batter becomes a runner, the inning ends, the batter is substituted for by a pinch-hitter or the pitcher incurs an injury. In the event a pitcher switches pitching hands during an at-bat because he has suffered an injury, the pitcher may not, for the remainder of the game, pitch with the hand from which he has switched. The

pitcher shall not be given the opportunity to throw any preparatory pitches after switching pitching hands. Any change of pitching hands must be indicated clearly to the umpire-in-chief."

It is interesting that a rather rare physical attribute was not so rare[1] that it could be ignored by the rules and left up to the umpire's discretion.

On almost the opposite side of the coin from Venditte is a player named Pete Gray. Pete played for only a single season in the majors in 1945. In 1923, Pete had an accident that changed his life dramatically. He fell off a wagon when he was only about 7 and got tangled in the spokes of the wagon's wheels.[2] The injury was to his right, dominant arm. When he was brought to the doctor the decision was made to amputate the arm above the elbow. This left Pete to relearn how to do everything as a lefty.

Pete's parents didn't baby him or treat him special because of the loss of his arm. It helped him to adjust and to build his confidence. He saw kids playing ball and started practicing on his own to develop his skills: swatting bottle caps and rocks with sticks. After some time he got up the confidence to ask to join in games. With time he learned to work around his limitations.

Gray's aspirations were like any kid's. He started to dream about playing big-league ball. When he was 17, he claims to have hitched rides to Chicago to see the World Series and said he was there for Ruth's called shot. He was inspired by Ruth's confidence.

He started playing in the church league and then caught on with a semi-pro team. Batting in a left-handed stance, he used a regular bat. Because it weighed 38 ounces, he bulked up his left arm lifting weights. He contributed regularly to the offense and defense and developed deft reflexes, skills, and techniques to compensate for having only one hand.

When the Japanese attacked Pearl Harbor in 1941, Pete wanted to enlist but was rejected because of his missing limb. He stuck to playing ball as people around his age were getting drafted or volunteered and the competition became a little less skilled.

"If I could teach myself how to play baseball with one arm, I sure as hell could handle a rifle."

— PETE GRAY

He was fast on the base paths and stole 68 bases for the Memphis Chickasaws in 1944—probably his best year in pro ball. He batted .333, hit 5 home runs, and struck out only 12 times in over 500 at-bats. The steals, average, and home runs didn't translate to his upcoming rookie year in the majors, but his performance with the Chickasaws caught the attention of the St. Louis Browns, and they signed him to a major league contract.

Pete did not like to be pitied for his injury because he didn't pity himself—and he let people know. Some of Gray's teammates—particularly pitchers Sig Jakucki and Nelson Potter—were constantly ragging him. Jakucki once put a dead fish in the pocket of Gray's new sports coat and Gray knocked him down with one punch. Considering that Pete worked his one arm out hard, he probably packed a wallop!

The war came to an end after the 1945 season, and all the talent started filtering back from the war. Pete held his own in the majors, but his .218 average was not enough to keep him in contention for a position and they let him go. He continued to play for years in the semi-pro leagues but never got back to the level of play he had shown promise of in 1944. But in that year, he played in eight games at Yankee Stadium and achieved an almost impossible dream.

"The only thing I wanted to do when I was a kid was play in Yankee Stadium and that came true."

— PETE GRAY

People all across the US heard about Pete, and he served as inspiration for troops who returned home as amputees. They saw what could be accomplished if they chose a goal and stuck with it. Gray was happy to contribute something to the veterans as he was not able to contribute by serving with them in the war.

"Maybe I wouldn't have done as well [if I had two arms]. I probably wouldn't have been as determined."

— PETE GRAY

1. As of this writing, eight pitchers have pitched in the majors who were ambidextrous. The only other in the modern era was Greg Harris who pitched to only two players with his left arm in his fifteen-year career. He did this in his final appearance in the majors.
2. Not only do the accounts of this vary, but what happened isn't clear either.

23

ESCAPE FROM CUBA

I t is rare to think of baseball in the context of international intrigue. When a baseball player's life is tied to human trafficking, bribery, blackmail, kidnapping, imprisonment, and illegally crossing borders, that opens a floodgate to the underworld. A sad reality, when compared to the freedoms that most of the world may enjoy, is the fate of players trapped in their homeland of Cuba.

Players in Cuba play for the love of the game or with the secret desire to someday defect and make a relative fortune overseas. It certainly is not for the meager pay. Under Fidel Castro, players who defected from Cuba and sought asylum in other countries were never able to return. This mostly affected players after 1959, when relations between the US and Cuba became strained during the cold war. The ultimate punishment for defection ended up being that players had to leave behind the world they knew and adopt a completely new way of life.

For defectors, this could mean leaving behind a wife and children, risking their lives or internment if they were captured, and a continued threat to their well-being even if they were successful. Essentially, defection became a dangerous race to escape capture and find sanctuary. The risks do not stop there as players may not have an immediate network of support, money, a contract, or certain success. Even some of the best players were not willing to risk these challenges and potential hardships.

A representative case of those willing to risk the difficulties is Yasiel Puig. A star in his homeland and somewhat reluctant to leave because of the dangers, Puig attempted defection thirteen times, each time putting him at greater potential for more extreme punishments. In his final try, he experienced a harrowing month-long journey to arrive in the USA.[1] Once there in 2012, he soon found himself a multi-millionaire in a very public spotlight.

Within his first five games in the majors, he hit 4 home runs and knocked in 10 RBI. By the end of the season he was batting .319 with 19 home runs in 382 at-bats, and he'd taken fan favor by storm. He was entertaining to watch and often humorous. While Puig got to enjoy his early success, the initial love affair began to wear off and his charm began to tarnish. His work ethic came into question as he did not show up to games on time, failed to give his full effort on the field, and eventually began showing aggression in starting fights.

A lot of this difficulty may simply have been that Puig was not adjusting well to the expectations of his teams, his teammates, and the culture he may have been reluctant to fully adopt. Having the privilege of riches at a young age and being enveloped in extravagance and abundance that had never been a part of his life could also have contributed. He has found himself bounced between teams who do not want the responsibility of handling his behavior.

Age and maturity may have mellowed Puig in time to give him another shot at reviving his career. He made a plea to baseball and the players' union in 2021:

Latino players do not understand what is expected of us as public figures in the USA. We need to learn English as well as understand American values and social norms. I cannot change the past, but I am determined to become a better person and I want to help other Latino players step into their roles successfully. The media pushed certain narratives about me because it sold more newspapers. They didn't understand my challenges or my culture or how that played an important role in my behavior. I also didn't know how to help them understand.[2]

Puig clearly had trouble with his adjustment, seeing his initial success deflate. If it was due to his inability to integrate with the sport smoothly and adapt to unwritten rules of the game and culture, this can be his opportunity to make a difference.

Should major league baseball accept his challenge to improve and adopt a better global strategy, it could put an end to dangerous trafficking, risky defections, and end the plight of players having to give up their homeland to enjoy their prominence as major league sports figures. Baseball could become a strategic component as a global ambassador not only for the sport but also for international relations. Maybe Puig will have a chance to reset his own compass and lead the way.

———————————————

1. There is no reason to repeat what is well-documented by ESPN : http://www.espn.com/espn/feature/story/_/id/10781144/no-one-walks-island-los-angeles-dodgers-yasiel-puig-journey-cuba
2. Paraphrased from Puig's message to MLB.

24

FIVE-FINGERED DISCOUNT ON THE RUN

For all the glam of powering a home run, in the end it is just numbers changing on the scoreboard. With a home run, the batter swings, the ball goes far, and the player jogs lazily around the bases while the players in the field yawn. So does the crowd. There is not really a strategy except for the normal interaction between the pitcher and batter. A home run can happen in any at-bat. The only people who seem to have fun are the players high-fiving each other in the dugout. An exception to the sleepy ritual of rounding the bases is a bat flip that upsets the other team, but the "unwritten rules" frown on that in an effort to homogenize the showmanship of that bit of fun.

Slick base running, on the other hand, always seems to stir up excitement in a game. There is charm in a smooth move, a bold one, or a brash one. Running the bases is an art of awareness, guile, and baseball savvy. It is a tool distinctly different than the big brawn that is commonly related to substance abuse. Players who use the base paths to make something happen to rally the fans and their team seem to be more inherently interesting. Ty Cobb obviously agrees.

There are a lot of naughty things some players manage in shaking up pitchers and the defense. The apex of that hunt for glory is stealing home. In stealing home, the situation is everything. No one is going to steal home with a ten-run lead or behind by that many. It only happens when runs are critical.

Situations for stealing home happen in two ways: a straight steal or a special play.

Special plays are more theatrics than cunning, although there are some elements of both. This can be when there are less than two out and the offense puts a squeeze play on that the batter tries to bunt and misses. Or, in a situation where it is first and third and there are opportunities to fluster the defense and force a mistake.[1]

A straight steal is when a player is on third or the bases are loaded or it is second and third and there is no sacrifice play on. The idea is, the runner on third is getting no help except for beating the throw from the pitcher to the plate. In this case, the runner at third has to be aware of all his advantages. He must see where the third baseman is and if he is being held. He has to know the pitcher's delivery. He has to be aware of his own skills. He has to know what the competition knows about him. He can use what he knows to his advantage, just as the defense can work against him.

There is a moment when these factors merge into the sublime.[2]

Let's set the stage. A third-string catcher with fewer than one hundred major league at-bats comes to the plate with one out in the bottom of the twelfth in a 4 to 4 tie. He hits a single. Willie McGee follows him with a single, Julio Gonzalez pops out for the second out, and Ozzie Smith hits the third single of the inning to load the bases. Bases loaded. Two out. Scrub catcher as the lead runner at third.

The mighty David Green steps up to the plate. He is batting .339 on that day for that season. It is his rookie year and he already has one hit in the game. The count gets to 1 ball and 2 strikes, but something is playing behind the scenes. With two out and the bases loaded, the Giants are looking for a force play at any base to end the inning. The infielders play back because all they need to do is field a ball cleanly. On a force out, no run will score. A swing and miss or strike looking sends the game into the thirteenth inning with the resolution still up in the air. The odds of seeing the top of the thirteenth inning are very high.

The lefty pitcher is not really paying attention to a catcher on third base.[3] Since when do rookie third-string catchers steal home? Darrell Evans is so far back from the third-base bag he is defending, he is practically playing left field. Glenn Brummer crept down the line with each pitch in the at-bat, testing to see if he could draw a throw. By the time the count was 1 and 2 he was leading a third of the way down the line.

The lefty started his delivery with the same high leg-kick he used on previous pitches, Brummer broke toward the plate. Infielders yelled out that the runner was breaking. Green stepped out of the batter's box. The ump jumped into position to call the play as Milt May, the catcher, stepped up out of the catcher's box before the ball left the pitcher's hand. May caught the ball and tried to put down the tag, but Brummer beat Lavelle's throw to home and the umpire called the runner safe. The Cardinals won the game 5 to 4 with 2 out in the twelfth on Brummer's steal of home. That is how it is in the record book.

No one was right. Everyone botched the play except Brummer.

The steal of home was already something that was already incredibly rare. But there was something unique to this. The third baseman was not paying attention. The pitcher was not paying attention. No one gave the steal sign. The third-string catcher on third running the bases—as slow as catchers are—never should have been going anywhere. And yet he was. Then the defensive catcher stepped out of the catcher's box on a routine pitch before it left the pitcher's hand. The ump stepped out of his position to call the live play, which was technically already dead. He called the sliding runner safe. It appeared he was.

But, wait… was the pitch a ball or a strike? Green didn't swing so if the pitch was a strike the third out was made and the run didn't count. Or was it the case that the ball was in play and the run scored before the pitch needed to be called?

This is messy. The timing of everything was in fractions of a second.

Had the tag been placed on Brummer, he probably should have been called safe because May stepped out of the catcher's box causing a very rare phenomenon known as a catcher's balk, Rule 5.02(a):

Except when the batter is being given an intentional base on balls, the catcher must stand with both feet within the lines of the catcher's box until the ball leaves the pitcher's hand.

The balk would have advanced all runners and the ball would be dead while scoring the winning run. Had May received the pitch and not caused the balk by stepping out of the catcher's box, the only thing that would have pushed the game into the thirteenth inning was if the pitch was called a strike before Brummer crossed the plate. But, if Brummer crossed the plate before the ball did, he scored the winning run before the pitch even needed to be called. Video shows he touched the plate before anything else mattered.[4]

Brummer had only one other steal that season. It was after he hit a double. He stole third and then scored on a sacrifice bunt. That means he was already flying toward home as the pitcher was releasing the ball, just like on the other steal of home.

This chapter should have been full of ultimate thieves and renegade runners like Jackie Robinson, Ty Cobb, Rickey Henderson, Lou Brock, Oscar Charleston, Tim

Raines, Turkey Stearnes, and Cool Papa Bell. Instead, you get a third-string catcher making a moment into the potato of his career on the major league stage. A catcher stealing home that won a game and maybe gave that small incentive to his team to take the division by just three games.

The Cardinals went on to win the World Series in 1982 and Glenn Brummer got a World Series ring. It may have all been on account of his brave swipe of home and one of the ultimate steals in the history of the game.

"Faster than that."

— BUCK O'NEIL WHEN ASKED HOW
FAST COOL PAPA BELL WAS RUNNING
THE BASES

---

1. There is an example of a failed attempt at this in chapter 4 "Jakey, the Sauerkraut-Faced Boob."
2. To be sure the usage of the word is clear, the definition is "to convert (something inferior) into something of higher worth."— Merriam-Webster dictionary
3. The record for stolen bases by a catcher in post-1900 play is held by Roger Bresnahan. Yes, a relative of the guy who had his number

retired in the minor leagues because he threw a potato to the third baseman.

4. A somewhat humorous recounting by Brummer of the event that he gets completely right and wrong at the same time. https://youtu.be/0turz4E5zxU

25

CALLED ON ACCOUNT OF CHAOS

There have been a lot of rare things in the previous twenty-four chapters of this book, including balking in runs, an outfielder with one arm, potatoes being swapped for baseballs, platinum sombreros, base-running gaffs, and a girl in the majors. There is no shortage of stars, personalities, dominance, strange plays, and extremes.

One very famous tale has a defining moment. The funny thing is the defining moment is the only part that gets remembered and the outcome is practically forgotten. The event includes two protests of the same game —made on separate days. A player was effectively traded in the middle of the game, somehow ending up 950 miles away between the second and third out in the top of the ninth inning. Almost 34,000 fans were at the game but only about 1,000 saw the final four outs.

Welcome to the Pine Tar Incident.

On July 24, 1983, the Yankees were playing the Royals in a Sunday afternoon game at Yankee stadium. The Yankees were leading 4 to 3 in the ninth when the Royals came to bat. Dale Murray had been pitching since the top of the sixth and only let up one hit. He got the first two Royals out,[1] then let up a single to U. L. Washington on a 0 and 2 count on a hard ground ball up the middle. Billy Martin, on his third tour as manager of the Bronx Bombers, decided to put in his closer, Goose Gossage, to finish off the game.

George Brett, a feared hitter batting .357 at the time of the game, stepped in and ripped the first pitch into the opposite field stands, but foul. The second pitch was not so lucky. Brett pulled a high fastball into the right-field seats for a home run. That gave the Royals a 5 to 4 lead. At least it seemed to be the apparent outcome at the time. The pitcher pitched, the batter swung and the ball went over the wall in fair territory. Pretty obvious to everyone who was watching. But this is baseball.

Billy Martin came out of the dugout calling the umpire's attention to something. The umpires convened making a fuss about inspecting the bat Brett had just used to hit the home run. Umpire Tim McClelland, a six-foot-six giant of a man walked with the bat and laid it across the width of the plate apparently measuring something. After a brief reconvene with the other umpires, still holding the bat, he took a few steps toward the Royals dugout, pointed to Brett, held up his fist, and called Brett out. So much for that home run. So much for that win. So much for what seemed to have happened just a moment ago.

Pandemonium ensued. Brett broke out of the dugout where he had been sitting calmly a moment before, totally enraged, swinging his arms over his head like a charging gorilla and having to be restrained as he thrashed like a madman in pursuit of McClelland. Gaylord Perry made off with the bat and handed it to someone who fled with it down into the tunnel of the visitor's dugout. The official call on the play was that Brett was using a bat where the pine tar was applied illegally. For that reason, he was called out.

In any case, the call had been made, it was the final out. People began filing out of the stadium because the Yankees had just won 4 to 3. Eventually, things calmed down on the field. Game over. That's where the story usually stops and so does the broadcast of the game. Most people who know the story might still think the Yankees won.

But that's really not exactly what happened. A much more rare and unusual thing occurred.

The Royals put the game under protest. Protests are usually just symbolic. Fans who see a manager protest a game see an umpire make a big "P" in the air and think to themselves "Yeah, right. Much ado about nothing." And it is rightly so because one thing more rare than a perfect game is a protest that affects the outcome of a game.

Four days later, that very rare thing that never really happens in baseball happened: the Royals' protest was upheld. Lee McPhail, the baseball commissioner, determined that the pine tar did not contribute to the home run. The rule had been put in place to keep balls from becoming discolored during play,[2] and as the ball left the ballpark, the pine tar had no effect on the pitch, the swing, the trajectory, or the outcome of the game.

With the call reversed, the game now stood with a score of Royals 5 Yankees 4. As the Royals still had one out left and the Yankees needed to bat in the ninth, the rest of the game had to be rescheduled to play at least the rest of the 4 outs that were still to be had by both teams in the game.

The Yankees and Royals both had days off on August 18 later that season. The Yankees were currently on a homestand and the Royals were scheduled to play in Baltimore the next day of their road trip so the meeting on that date was convenient. After some haggling about fan entrance to the game,[3] play was set to resume in front of what was estimated to be a whopping crowd of more than 1,000 fans.

Billy Martin knew he'd have to score at least one run, so he made a few slick moves in his lineup to get his bats in line and allow some flexibility as to where to slot his pinch-hitters. One issue he also had to cover was that Jerry Mumphrey had been traded to Houston on August 10, so was not able to resume play. He was no longer on the team.

Hal McRae who had been due up to hit twenty-five days earlier stepped in to hit and the pitcher, George Frazier, toed the rubber. Frazier then immediately stepped off. He turned and threw the ball to Ken Griffey who was playing first base in an appeal. The umpire, who had not seen the play, called Brett—who was not even in the stadium—safe.

Griffey threw the ball back to Frazier who again toed the rubber, stepped off, and then threw the ball to Roy Smalley at second base. It was another appeal play, and the second-base umpire, who was also not in the ball-park on the day that the game was played, called Brett and U.L. Washington safe.

This was a shrewd move by Martin, as the umpiring crew was different than the crew who worked the game on July 24. Billy came out of the dugout and questioned the umpires as to how they could possibly make calls on a game they did not even attend. Somehow, they produced paperwork that apparently had an affidavit from the previous crew. Nevertheless, Martin put the game under protest again. McRae proceeded to strike out on six pitches to end the seemingly endless inning.

It would be nice if that were the end of the complexity.

Don Mattingly stepped up for the Yankees with a very strange hitting streak on the line. He had hit in fourteen straight games before the game on July 24 and then ten more afterward. The opportunity to come up and bat again and get a hit could connect the two streaks and set a new record for a rookie hitting in consecutive games.

Mattingly flew out to the disappointment of about 900 people—as even the few that were there had started to filter out of the stands—and the streak ended. Smalley got up and flew out. Oscar Gamble pinch-hit and grounded out to second ending the game. Dan Quisenberry, who had come on in relief for the Royals, notched his thirty-third save to lead the league. As it went, the interminable game ended for the fans, players, and announcers twenty-five days after it had begun as Martin's new protest came to nothing.

With the end of that game also came one of the rarest occurrences in baseball. The team that protested an event in a game not only won the protest but won the game as well. Like all mythic adventures of great heroes, the events of those days spawned at least two songs commemorating the days of battling heroes.[4]

---

1. Don Mattingly made a great play to stop an extra-base hit.
2. The most hysterical reason for any rule in baseball. It makes sense. But the next time I am pitching with the game on the line, I am wiping the ball on my face to pick up the eye-black paint so the spin confounds the batter. As far as our research team knows, that is something that never happened in the history of the game and may require a new rule.
3. This is actually funny. Fans who had tickets to the original game wanted to get in for free and the Yankee office wanted to charge $2.50 admission to get fans in the seats. At worst, any fan attending was looking at 4 outs. Never mind how much it took to park a car or travel to the stadium. If you look at the number of fans in the stands, the announcer even jokes that there are about thirty-two people in attendance. For both announcers it would be the shortest amount of time either one of them spent announcing a live game.
4. "The Ballad of George Brett," by The Barking Geckos (https://youtu.be/uMd5JdDg-Go) and "The Pine-Tarred Bat," by Dennis Reed Jr. (https://youtu.be/NgkXHK9li3c)

EXITING THE EXTREME STADIUM

As every game must see its final out, so we have come to the end of this outing. I hope it leaves readers with a kind of satisfaction and a feeling of richness in exploring the implications of the game.

The mighty depth of baseball lore is often hard to fathom in its complexity, tall tales, truths, and dreams. These stories hopefully helped fans perusing the pages to learn details about other dimensions of the game they did not know while paying homage to stories that are more familiar but of a sort that gets shared by generations of fans. In these stories, and the thousands not told here, baseball creates its own lasting legend through personality, situation, and suspense. The character and passion are more than just a swing or a pitch.

"Baseball is dull only to dull minds."

— RED BARBER

LEAVE A REVIEW

If you have enjoyed these tales and maybe even learned something, let me know. If the book has fulfilled its promise, please put up a review and spread the word to those who will enjoy it. I hope it will be possible to bring more stories to readers.

"I guess my thermometer for my baseball fever is still a goose bump." - Vin Scully

Scan the QR Code below to leave a Review!

mail: lingsterbooks@gmail.com

instagram: @roy_lingster

Facebook: Roy Lingster